Parish Guide to Implementing the

Roman Missal

Third Edition

COMMITTEE ON DIVINE WORSHIP
UNITED STATES CONFERENCE OF CATHOLIC BISHOPS

UNITED STATES CONFERENCE OF CATHOLIC BISHOPS
WASHINGTON, D.C.

The document *Parish Guide to Implementing the Roman Missal, Third Edition* was developed as a resource by the Committee on Divine Worship of the United States Conference of Catholic Bishops (USCCB). It was reviewed by the committee chairman, Bishop Arthur J. Serratelli, and has been authorized for publication by the undersigned.

Msgr. David J. Malloy, STD
General Secretary, USCCB

Scripture texts used in this work are taken from the *New American Bible*, copyright © 1991, 1986, and 1970 by the Confraternity of Christian Doctrine, Washington, DC 20017 and are used by permission of the copyright owner. All rights reserved.

Excerpts from the *Lectionary for Mass for Use in the Dioceses of the United States*, copyright © 2001, 1998, 1997, and 1970 by the Confraternity of Christian Doctrine, Washington, DC 20017, used with permission. All rights reserved. No portion of this text may be reproduced without permission in writing from the copyright holder.

Excerpts from the *Catechism of the Catholic Church*, second edition, copyright © 2000, Libreria Editrice Vaticana– United States Conference of Catholic Bishops, Washington, D.C. Used with permission. All rights reserved.

Excerpts from *Vatican Council II: The Conciliar and Post Conciliar Documents* edited by Austin Flannery, OP, copyright © 1975, Costello Publishing Company, Inc., Northport, NY, are used with permission of the publisher, all rights reserved. No part of these excerpts may be reproduced, stored in a retrieval system, or transmitted in any form or by any means—electronic, mechanical, photocopying, recording, or otherwise— without express written permission of Costello Publishing Company.

Excerpts from Pope Benedict XVI, *Sacramentum Caritatis*, copyright © 2007, Libreria Editrice Vaticana (LEV), Vatican City; excerpts from Pope Benedict XVI, *The Eucharist* (Spiritual Thoughts Series), copyright © 2009, LEV. Used with permission; all rights reserved.

Excerpts from the English translation of the *General Instruction of the Roman Missal* ©2010, International Commission on English in the Liturgy, Inc. (ICEL); excerpts from the English translation of *The Roman Missal* © 2010, ICEL. All rights reserved.

Excerpts from *Liturgiam Authenticam: Fifth Instruction on Vernacular Translation of the Roman Liturgy* © 2001, United States Conference of Catholic Bishops. All rights reserved.

Cover Photo: Holy Name Cathedral, Chicago (CNS/Karen Callaway).

ISBN 978-1-60137-093-8

First printing, October 2010

Copyright © 2010, United States Conference of Catholic Bishops, Washington, D.C. All rights reserved. No part of this work may be reproduced or transmitted in any form or by any means, electronic or mechanical, including photocopying, recording, or by any information storage and retrieval system, without permission in writing from the copyright holder.

CONTENTS

PART III: AN IN-DEPTH IMPLEMENTATION PROCESS

LIST OF ABBREVIATIONS

CCC	*Catechism of the Catholic Church*
CCMA	Catholic Campus Ministry Association
FDLC	Federation of Diocesan Liturgical Commissions
GIRM	*General Instruction of the Roman Missal*
LFM	*Lectionary for Mass*
NADDCM	National Association of Diocesan Directors of Campus Ministry
NCCL	National Conference for Catechetical Leadership
NCEA	National Catholic Educational Association
NFCYM	National Federation for Catholic Youth Ministry
NOCERCC	National Organization for Continuing Education of Roman Catholic Clergy
NPM	National Association of Pastoral Musicians
SC	*Constitution on the Sacred Liturgy (Sacrosanctum Concilium)*
USCCB	United States Conference of Catholic Bishops

PREFACE

Dear brothers and sisters in Christ:

"It is truly right to give you thanks, truly just to give you glory, Father most holy." These words from the Preface of the newly translated Eucharistic Prayer IV express what is essential and unchanging about our participation in these sacred mysteries.

Nearly forty years have passed since the translation of the first edition of the *Missale Romanum*. During that time, our liturgical experience has deepened our faith, nurtured our hope, and become an instrument through which we celebrate God's gift of eternal life to us through the Incarnation, Passion, Death, and Resurrection of Jesus Christ. This history and our theological reflection also allow us to acknowledge the inadequacies in the text that is widely used in the English-speaking world. With the fifth instruction *Liturgiam Authenticam*, His Holiness Pope John Paul II provided a means for us to reclaim the theological richness of the words of the Holy Sacrifice of the Mass.

The same Council that brought us the initial translation of the Mass also called upon the Church to embrace her roles and responsibilities in her participation in these sacred mysteries. With this revised translation of the third edition of the *Missale Romanum*, we have an opportunity to embrace again the Church's earnest desire that all the faithful should be led to fully conscious and active participation in the Liturgy (see Second Vatican Council, *Constitution on the Sacred Liturgy* [*Sacrosanctum Concilium*], no. 14).

The resources in the *Parish Guide to Implementing the Roman Missal, Third Edition*, have been developed to provide parishes with a road map for promoting and implementing these newly translated texts and for catechizing the faithful about them. This *Parish Guide* builds on the bishops' priority initiatives to deepen faith, nurture hope, and celebrate life with practical guidelines and tools for parish leaders to use in their remote and proximate catechesis on the texts and the Mass.

We hope that the extensive work of all those involved in the process of translation and preparation of this *Parish Guide* will bear abundant fruit in the vibrant and authentic worship of the Church.

Sincerely yours in Christ,

+ Arthur J. Serratelli

Most Rev. Arthur J. Serratelli
Bishop of Paterson
Chairman, Committee on Divine Worship
United States Conference of Catholic Bishops

INTRODUCTION

A. GETTING STARTED

1. Purpose of the *Parish Guide*

For the goal of apostolic endeavor is that all who are made sons [and daughters] of God by faith and baptism should come together to praise God in the midst of his Church, to take part in the Sacrifice and to eat the Lord's Supper.

> —Second Vatican Council,
> *Constitution on the Sacred Liturgy*
> (*Sacrosanctum Concilium* [SC]), no. 10[1]

Almost fifty years ago, the Council Fathers envisioned a renewal of the Eucharist that would draw Catholics together to worship and praise God in fullness of body, mind, and heart. The Council Fathers desired that the baptized would earnestly come to the sacraments in search of holiness and the grace that flows from the mercy and love of God alone.

Since the promulgation of the first translation of the Mass into the vernacular in the 1970s, the world—including the world of texts and translation—has seen many changes. Scholastic advancements, especially in the area of translation, have revealed the inadequacies of the current texts that we use at Mass. The *Roman Missal, Third Edition*, is the result of the Church's efforts to better communicate the mysteries of salvation that we celebrate at Mass.

The purpose of this *Parish Guide* is to provide parish leaders—clergy, staff, and volunteers—with

- A vision, goals, and objectives for implementing the *Roman Missal*
- Planning and organizational resources that you can use to create a successful plan for implementing the changes in accord with your parish's particular needs
- Practical tools and suggested activities in diverse formats—print, audio, video, and Web—and for various groups—parishioners, catechists, youth, and musicians—that you can use as provided or adapted for your parish situation

This *Parish Guide* also will direct you to a wealth of additional resources that are available online and from other publishers to complement the tools included here.

---

1 See Second Vatican Council, *Constitution on the Sacred Liturgy* (*Sacrosanctum Concilium*), in *Vatican Council II: Volume 1: The Conciliar and Post-Conciliar Documents*, ed. Austin Flannery (Northport, NY: Costello Publishing, 1996).

We hope that this copy of the *Parish Guide* eventually will be only a cover with a few pages left, because

✠ Everything on the to-do list has been checked off.
✠ All liturgical ministers have been trained and renewed in their ministry.
✠ Every handout and worksheet has been copied and used by staff and committees.
✠ Every resource, regardless of format, has been shared widely with parishioners as your parish works toward fulfilling the hunger that draws us to the Lord's table, where we are nurtured to do justice and perform acts of charity among the least of our brothers and sisters.

At the end of this Introduction you will find more information about this *Parish Guide*, including a practical overview of its structure and suggested approaches for using it to implement the *Roman Missal*, in your parish or school.

2. Deepen, Nurture, Celebrate

In November 2009, the bishops of the United States approved a pastoral plan to guide their collaborative work for the coming years. The theme of this plan is "Deepen Faith. Nurture Hope. Celebrate Life."

One of the priority goals of the bishops' pastoral plan is to prepare for the implementation of the *Roman Missal*. It is easy to see this goal's close relationship to the plan's theme. Preparing for the *Roman Missal* is not simply a matter of buying new books and learning to recite and sing revised texts. It is an opportunity to examine and renew our celebration and understanding of the Eucharistic Liturgy that stands at the heart of Christian life.

The revised translation of the Liturgy will deepen faith by using words and images that draw on the Church's rich theological Tradition. It will nurture Christian hope for the day when we may celebrate the wedding feast of the Lamb at the table of the Lord in heaven. It will celebrate the boundless love of God, shown most profoundly in the

Paschal Mystery of Jesus Christ, celebrated and made present in the Eucharistic Liturgy. This period of implementation offers an opportunity to deepen our understanding and appreciation of the Liturgy, nurture liturgical practices that will lead to fuller liturgical participation, and celebrate the Liturgy with renewed purpose.

Those charged with implementing the *Roman Missal* will need to follow the example of "the head of a household who brings from his storeroom both the new and the old" (Mt 13:52). Implementing the revised text is not a rejection of the last forty (or four hundred) years of liturgical practice. It is an opportunity for deeper understanding, greater attention to words and gestures, and more intentional participation. The renewed Liturgy will help form disciples who live in communion with God and each other—disciples who live a Christian life.

Implementing the *Roman Missal* requires a period of catechesis for the whole parish community. It will not be enough for the priests to practice the revised prayer texts and the choir to learn revised musical settings. Every member of the parish should understand not only the content of the changes (the revised prayer texts) but also the reasons underlying these changes. Only then will this implementation bring us closer to the goal stated by the Fathers of the Second Vatican Council: the "full, conscious, and active participation" of all the faithful in the liturgical action (SC, no. 14).

This participation is essential if the renewal of the Liturgy is to be accomplished, because a liturgical congregation is not an audience that is handed a program to follow in which they play a limited part. As the Council Fathers said,

> On the contrary, through a good understanding of the rites and prayers they should take part in the sacred action, conscious of what they are doing, with devotion and full collaboration. They should be instructed by God's word, and be nourished at the table of the Lord's Body. They should give thanks to God. Offering

the immaculate victim, not only through the hands of the priest but also together with him, they should learn to offer themselves. Through Christ, the Mediator, they should be drawn day by day into ever more perfect union with God and each other, so that finally God may be all in all. (SC, no. 48)

For the faithful, liturgical participation is grounded in Baptism. Conformed to Christ in this sacrament, the faithful "share in the priesthood of Christ, in his prophetic and royal mission" (*Catechism of the Catholic Church* [CCC], no. 1268).[2] Furthermore, full, conscious, and active liturgical participation means living the great commandment given to us by the Lord: "you shall love the Lord, your God, with all your heart, with all your soul, and with all your mind" (Mt 22:37). Participation in the Liturgy with all our heart, mind, and soul is the goal to which we should aspire so that, united with Christ in the Holy Spirit, we may make an acceptable sacrifice to the Father.

Fostering active participation in the Liturgy extends beyond knowing what to say and when to sit or stand or kneel. Active participation must be both interior and exterior. Through our catechetical efforts—both before the implementation and in the months and years after—the ministers and the faithful must grow in their understanding of the meaning of these revised texts through worthy celebration of the Eucharistic Liturgy and through private meditation and reflection on the texts and actions of that Liturgy. Active participation in the Liturgy is a fundamental disposition that flows into a way of life. Those who take an active part in the Liturgy should go out from the congregation conscious of their responsibility to proclaim the message they have just celebrated. The heart and mind must be in harmony with what is proclaimed with the lips. Only then will this time of catechesis **deepen** our participation in the Lord's sacrifice and **nurture** our Christian commitment, so that we may **celebrate** forever at the table of the Lamb.

3. Reasons to Implement the *Roman Missal*

The Eucharistic Liturgy is the center of the Church's life. In this Liturgy, the whole Body of Christ gathers around its head, Jesus Christ, to join with his perfect sacrifice of praise and thanksgiving to the Father. In receiving the Eucharist, we receive strength to grow more like Christ and lead lives of loving service, conformed to him.

Given liturgy's importance, it is no surprise that the first document of the Second Vatican Council addressed the Sacred Liturgy. The *Constitution on the Sacred Liturgy* authorized the reform of the Mass and the sacraments and allowed broader use of the vernacular in liturgical celebrations. The *Missale Romanum* containing the reformed Order of Mass was published in 1970. The English translation was approved by the National Conference of Catholic Bishops in 1973, and the Sacramentary was published in 1974. The second Latin edition was published in 1975 and was incorporated into the Sacramentary in 1985. To celebrate the Jubilee Year in 2000, Pope John Paul II authorized the third edition of the Latin *Missale Romanum*, and preparation of an English translation of the third edition began.

In 2001, the Congregation for Divine Worship and the Discipline of the Sacraments issued *Liturgiam Authenticam*, an instruction regarding the preparation of translations of liturgical texts. Looking back at thirty years' experience of vernacular liturgy, *Liturgiam Authenticam* issued new guidelines for liturgical translations, including the new English translation of the *Roman Missal*. In accord with these guidelines, the new translation is more literal and comes closer to the original Latin texts in style and structure. The translation uses more formal language that better reflects allusions from Scripture and patristic thought, creating a liturgical language that reflects the dignity of the Sacred Liturgy.

This new liturgical language will be different from the language used in ordinary conversation. It uses words filled with theological meaning, drawing on the depths of Scripture and the Church's rich Tra-

---

2 *Catechism of the Catholic Church*, 2nd ed. (Washington, DC: Libreria Editrice Vaticana—United States Conference of Catholic Bishops [USCCB], 2000).

dition. As a result, this language may seem unfamiliar and even awkward to many parishioners. Many may find it disconcerting to pray revised texts that replace those long ago committed to memory. A parish-wide catechetical process can help alleviate some of the unease that is likely. If done well, with care and intention, this catechesis can lead to a renewed understanding and appreciation of the Eucharistic Liturgy and its foundational role in the Christian life.

Catechesis for the *Roman Missal* will touch every element of parish life. Priests and the faithful will learn to pray the revised texts well. Musicians will learn new settings of the sung parts of the Mass. Catechists and teachers will help children and adults understand the revised texts. When we take the time to work together to develop and implement a parish plan, implementing the *Roman Missal* can become an opportunity to renew our celebration and appreciation of the Liturgy. We can come to the celebration more mindfully, aware of the importance of this work uniting heaven and earth. We can be more conscious of the words we address to God, reflecting more deeply on the meaning of the words we pray. Through prayer and study of these revised texts, we can enter more deeply into our faith. By confronting unfamiliar words, such as "consubstantial" and "ineffable," we can study the concepts that underlie them, growing in knowledge of our faith. By reflecting on the scriptural allusions in the revised prayers, we can increase our familiarity with the Word of God contained in Sacred Scripture and come to a renewed appreciation of the close relationship between Scripture and the Liturgy.

Although many in the Church have eagerly anticipated the revised texts, some parishes may face resistance to the *Roman Missal*. Some people may not like the revised translations. Others may express concern that comprehensive catechesis about the revised missal will distract from the other important work of the parish. Some may even wonder how parishes will afford new ritual books, hymnals, and musical settings. Parish leaders will have to address these concerns head-on—recognizing the real fear that underlies them, but helping the parish to move past these concerns and obstacles to a deeper and more meaningful liturgical prayer.

By participating in this nationwide effort of liturgical catechesis, we will experience anew the importance of communion and of being one with the Church. We celebrate the Eucharistic Liturgy not as individuals, but as one Church, gathered as the Body of Christ. Our celebration is diminished if each member of that Body does not participate in the Liturgy with heart, mind, and soul. As the *Constitution on the Sacred Liturgy* states, the goal is the "full, conscious, and active participation" of all the faithful (SC, no. 14). In accord with the liturgical role each of us may play (celebrant, lector, musician, altar server, congregation member, and so on), we must enter into the Eucharistic Liturgy fully. Interior as well as exterior participation is the goal, and that goal requires careful preparation and catechesis.

4. ABCs of a Successful Preparatory Period

As you consider how best to begin planning to implement the *Roman Missal,* use the ABCs—**attract**, **build**, and **create**—as starting points:

Attract the right people to the team.

Build understanding, energy, and enthusiasm for the Mass.

Create your parish plan.

ATTRACT the Right People to the Team

The key to any successful pastoral strategy or ministry is the people who are involved. Remember, our greatest asset is people—we who make up the Body of Christ here on earth.

Therefore, as your parish or school community begins planning, the first step is to identify the key people who should be involved and to secure their participation. Because the liturgical life of the community affects so many areas of church life, a broad cross-section of ministries and ministers, both volunteer and paid, should be invited to participate. Leaders in key ministries and their related parish or school committees include

⍟ Pastoral life
⍟ Parish or school administration

✠ Liturgy and music
✠ Religious education or religion
✠ Youth ministry
✠ Campus ministry

See Worksheet 1—Roles and Responsibilities for a more detailed list about whom you might invite to serve on the planning and implementation team and their potential responsibilities.

Choose one person to be the lead coordinator or facilitator for the planning team. This person is not necessarily the decision maker—rather, he or she is someone who will stay on top of the various planning activities.

Review the roles and responsibilities of each person on the planning team. Take time to clarify who has decision-making responsibilities and how decisions for the implementation will be made, both for the parish or school as a whole and for specific ministries. For example, will the staff decide which resources should be used to support the implementation (e.g., hymnals and catechetical resources), or does the planning team want to make that decision?

BUILD Understanding, Energy, and Enthusiasm for the Mass: Have the Right Attitude

Use the materials throughout this guide to develop a greater understanding among parish staff and lay leaders, and then among parishioners in general. When meeting with the planning team, express an engaging vision, with a positive attitude, about implementing and understanding the revised translations. You may want to use the information provided in this guide, along with materials on the *Roman Missal* Web site of the United States Conference of Catholic Bishops (USCCB) (*www.usccb.org/romanmissal*), to develop this vision.

Here are some pointers to guide you toward the right approach:

✠ Be **positive** about the revised translation, the planning and implementation process, and the potential impact on the liturgical life of the parish.

✠ Be **clear** about how the implementation will take place, what roles parish members will play, and how parishioners can get involved.
✠ Be **proactive** by anticipating questions and concerns that parish leaders and parishioners might have about the revised translation of the Mass.
✠ Be **sensitive** to parishioners' responses to the changes.
✠ Be **patient** as the parish makes and implements these changes.

CREATE Your Parish Plan

Begin by discussing with the parish staff and pastoral council how the parish can best prepare to implement the *Roman Missal*. Talk about ways to enhance the liturgical life of the parish and deepen understanding and appreciation of the Mass. Your parish or school can plan for a successful implementation by developing an intentional plan of action for welcoming the *Roman Missal*. This *Parish Guide* includes a planning process and contains worksheets and handouts to facilitate effective planning. See Part I for a discussion on developing a basic Action Plan that you can use to get started. Part III provides a process for a more in-depth approach to planning.

B. GOALS AND OBJECTIVES FOR THE IMPLEMENTATION

The implementation of the revised translation of the *Roman Missal* can have several goals. This book addresses two overall goals that are supported by the resources in this guide:

Goal 1. To provide parish leaders with the appropriate concrete resources to plan and implement a parish-wide program of liturgical formation and catechesis on the newly translated Mass

Goal 2. To help the faithful participate more fully, actively, and consciously in the Mass

Goal 1 lies at the heart of this guide, because the responsibility to breathe life into the revised translations will rest largely with the parish. Some objectives to support Goal 1 are as follows:

✠ To identify the roles and responsibilities of key leaders for the parish implementation
✠ To create a parish Action Plan (see page 8)
✠ To set a schedule for implementing the parish Action Plan
✠ To communicate with the parish about the parish's Action Plan and about the changes themselves
✠ To make print, audio, video, and online resources available to leaders and parishioners
✠ To train the trainers at the parish level through print, in-person, and online resources
✠ To develop camera-ready resources to promote general catechesis and liturgical formation on the changes in the Mass

Goal 2 takes its cue from the *Constitution on the Sacred Liturgy*, which identifies full and active participation as the Church's primary aim in liturgy. The implementation of the revised translation gives us a new and teachable opportunity, more than forty years after the Council, to inspire the community of faith to praise God together. Some objectives that flow from Goal 2 are as follows:

✠ To provide resources and tools to help the faithful practice the revised people's texts
✠ To train liturgical ministers to develop an increased sensitivity that allows them to lead the newly translated texts well
✠ To make connections, in preaching, between the newly translated texts and their scriptural roots as they appear naturally in the Lectionary cycle
✠ To plan opportunities for all parishioners to reflect on their roles as leaders of and participants in the Mass (e.g., as musicians, extraordinary ministers of the Eucharist, catechists, or parents)
✠ To encourage parish leaders (e.g., paid and volunteer catechists, youth ministers, and committee members) to plan and participate in sessions or experiences that focus on the Mass and their participation in it

These two goals and their objectives are starting points from which your parish can develop and refine more specific goals and objectives—and activities to implement them—that are particular and appropriate to the practices within your diocese and to the diversity and needs of your parish.

As you begin your pastoral planning, refer to these goals and objectives frequently, along with any planning resources developed by your bishop and diocesan staff. Together they can serve as the foundation of a practical, useful, and successful implementation plan.

C. USING THIS PARISH GUIDE: A PRACTICAL OVERVIEW

1. Structure of This *Parish Guide*

This *Parish Guide* is divided into three parts, plus appendices.

Part I of this resource is a simple planning guide that provides parish and school leaders with a concrete strategy for implementing the *Roman Missal*. It outlines a process that your parish and/or school can follow to discuss, identify, and create a plan of action.

Part II contains a sample calendar for implementation, as well as concrete suggestions and resources for general catechesis, training, and general ministry areas. These are all resources that you can use to implement your own Action Plan.

Part III, developed in a workbook format, provides a more detailed process that you can use to gather a team and create your own local plan. This Part also contains the forms and handouts needed to complete a parish Action Plan in greater depth for implementing the *Roman Missal*.

The **Appendices** have additional resources to support the implementation and your parish or school's adaptation of the strategies in this guide.

2. Two Approaches to Using the *Parish Guide*

A Simple Plan for Implementing the *Roman Missal*

If your parish or school has limited resources and time, you may want to focus on Parts I and II. Part I provides concrete tools to do a simple, straightforward implementation of the *Roman Missal*. The ready-made materials in Part II and the appendices will be very valuable for such an implementation strategy; you can use them as a menu of possible activities. Consider reviewing Part III to find other practical ideas for your implementation strategy, including useful handouts.

An In-Depth Implementation Plan for Deeper Renewal of Liturgical Life

If your parish or school has the interest, time, and resources to plan a deeper implementation process targeted at renewing your community's liturgical life, Part I may provide a general overview, but Part III is where you will find a detailed workbook with appropriate materials to guide you through the various steps of such a process. The ready-made materials in Part II and the appendices will be helpful in carrying out this deeper plan for renewal.

PART I

A SIMPLE PLANNING GUIDE

The purpose of Part I is to help your community to develop your own strategy for implementing the *Roman Missal, Third Edition,* and to renew liturgical life and spirituality. Part I is especially intended to provide a broad overview for those parishes and schools with limited time and resources to undertake an in-depth planning process.

Part I is organized into three sections: criteria for planning, a basic Action Plan, and a road map and planning calendar for both the remote and proximate preparation. Each section builds on the previous. After completing the activities outlined in this part, your community should have a road map for achieving your desired goals.

Note that the workbook section of this guide, Part III, discusses some of the same steps in greater depth, with additional planning materials and tools for those parishes and schools with sufficient resources and interest to plan a deeper implementation tailored to the community's needs.

A. CRITERIA FOR EFFECTIVE PLANNING

Effective pastoral planning for the implementation will do the following:

✠ **Provide an implementation strategy** and schedule.

✠ **Identify and clearly define desired outcomes** so that the pastoral plan can be effectively evaluated.

✠ **Identify resources to help leaders reflect** more deeply on the Eucharist, the *Roman Missal*, and their parish or school.

✠ **Identify resources to help leaders train** volunteers, especially in liturgical ministry.

✠ **Provide parishioners with print, audio, and online resources** that promote a deeper understanding of the Eucharist and the *Roman Missal*, and allow them to practice the people's parts.

✠ **Lead the parish or school community** to a greater participation in and appreciation of the Mass.

B. A BASIC ACTION PLAN

An effective Action Plan for implementing the *Roman Missal* will accomplish the following:

✠ Focus attention on specific and measurable goals.

✠ Highlight four to seven objectives for implementing the goals.

✠ Name and prioritize the activities that your parish or school will use to fulfill those objectives.

✠ Put each activity on an implementation calendar.

✠ Identify necessary resources including people to implement each activity.

Set a meeting place and time—1 ½ to 2 hours should be sufficient—and invite your planning team to the meeting. In preparation for the meeting, you might send them copies of the criteria (above) and the goals and objectives (page 5) to review ahead of time, or direct them to the Internet where they can download this information at *www.usccb.org/romanmissal*.

Draft and send out a basic agenda for the meeting like this one. Note that the majority of the time will be spent on the Action Plan.

1. Introductions
2. Review and approval of criteria
3. Review and selection of goals and objectives
4. Create an Action Plan

On the evening of the meeting, have copies of the criteria, the goals and objectives, Worksheet 5—Action Plan by Objective, and Worksheet 6—Twelve-Month Planning Calendar.

Criteria for Effective Planning

After brief introductions, review the criteria for effective planning from the beginning of this part. Because these criteria will guide your work on developing the Action Plan, take time to explore any questions or concerns that team members have. Since every parish or school is unique, solicit suggestions to modify, add to, or delete any criteria that do not match the needs or character of your parish or school. Ask the team to approve the criteria before moving on.

Goals and Objectives

The introduction highlighted two goals and a list of potential objectives (page 5) that could lead any parish or school to a successful implementation of the *Roman Missal*. Use these as a starting point for developing your own parish goals and corresponding objectives. Consider limiting the number of goals to two or three and the total number of objectives to four to seven. Using one copy of Worksheet 5—Action Plan by Objective, fill in the goal and objec-

tive section. During this step, identify a clear way to measure the outcome for each objective: how will you know that you have reached your objective?

Action Plan

Now that your team has identified goals and objectives for implementing the *Roman Missal*, how will your parish turn this vision into reality? The goals and objectives you have established should be the guide to planning. The next step is to identify the activities that your parish or school can do or already does that will help you meet each objective.

Using Worksheet 5—Action Plan by Objective, identify the current parish or school activities that fulfill the objective. Then, brainstorm additional activities that the parish or school could do. For each, note the start and end dates (timeline), what resources are needed (budget, people, space, materials), and who will be responsible for leading that activity.

Evaluate the activities: how well do they help you meet this objective? How well do they meet your planning criteria? Do you have the resources needed to make this activity happen? Make any changes that this evaluation reveals.

The last step is to put the activities of the Action Plan in the calendar (Worksheet 6—Twelve-Month Planning Calendar), noting their start and end dates. Certain time periods will naturally be busier, especially those months immediately preceding the first-use date. The timing of some activities may be more flexible, so negotiate any changes in the timeline with the team, and update your copies of Worksheet 5 as needed.

When your team has completed its work, take a few minutes to review the plan as a whole. Revisit the criteria for effective planning and assess your Action Plan. Does the plan you developed meet these criteria? Where are the gaps between criteria and plans? What might you need to change or add? Encourage your team to come up with ways to address any concerns that arise during this assessment and make the appropriate adjustments.

C. A ONE-YEAR ROAD MAP FOR LITURGICAL PREPARATION AND CATECHESIS

The following suggestions offer practical ways in which parishes can prepare to implement the *Roman Missal*.

This schedule suggests a two-pronged approach:

1. Preparing parish leaders and ministers

    *   Clergy (including deacons, visiting priests, and weekend assistants)
    *   Parish professional staff (e.g., school, religious education, liturgy, youth, social justice, and pastoral associates)
    *   Ministry leaders (from all parish ministries)

2. Preparing parishioners

    *   Use of homilies during Mass
    *   Use of present educational, catechetical, and other ministry opportunities

At a Glance: Parish Liturgical and Catechetical Road Map

The months are given in countdown order. Month 12 represents one year out from the date of first use of the *Roman Missal*. Month 1 represents the month of the first use.

✠ *January–March 2011*
Target the planning process: gathering the right people, studying documents, identifying a vision, developing goals and objectives, and finalizing an implementation plan.

✠ *April–August 2011*
Target implementation of the plan, including the education of parish leaders and the preparation of resources for parishioner use.

✠ *September–December 2011*
Target the proximate preparation of parishioners (adults, youth, and children) through a multistep process that begins with providing a series of adult education/formation sessions and homilies and with introducing new music. The goal is to have a well-formed congregation when the parish first begins to use the revised rite.

PART II

ACTIVITIES TO IMPLEMENT THE PLAN

Parishes and schools have a hectic schedule of activities that form the core of their ministry. Although the implementation of the *Roman Missal* will become a significant part of that schedule, it does not have to overwhelm the good and important work that is already taking place.

In Section A, you will find a sample "Parish Life Calendar" that identifies ways in which you can weave preparations to receive the *Roman Missal* into your present parish and school activities.

Section B, "Suggestions for Parishes and Schools," provides a list of activities that will help promote awareness and understanding of the revised translation in your parish. Some suggestions capitalize on widely used Internet technology, including Web sites, e-mail, and social networking sites. You can use the existing tools, resources, and activities as a menu of ideas, or you might adapt them to best meet the needs of your parishioners.

A. PARISH LIFE CALENDAR (SEPTEMBER 2011-JUNE 2012)

September 2011

Catechetical Sunday is celebrated on the third Sunday of September in most dioceses. Less than three months away from Advent and the implementation of the *Roman Missal*, this Sunday provides an excellent opportunity to begin catechizing the members of the parish about the changes in the Liturgy.

✠ Announce the parish program for liturgical catechesis in the bulletin and with signs around the parish grounds.
✠ Include all those involved in catechizing about the *Roman Missal* in the blessing of catechists.
✠ Hold back-to-school events for the parish school and religious education programs during this week. Emphasize the parents' role as the primary catechists of their children, and hand out cards with the revised Mass texts for parents to practice with their children.

✠ Consider using this Sunday's homilies to discuss the Liturgy as "the privileged place for catechizing the People of God" (CCC, no. 1074), stressing the importance of interior and exterior participation in the Liturgy as the foundation of well-formed faith and Christian living.

October 2011

Respect Life Month is celebrated all month, with a special emphasis on the first Sunday of October. Respect Life Month is an excellent opportunity to focus on the Body of Christ. In the Eucharist, we celebrate and bring about our oneness in Jesus Christ our Lord. This oneness extends to all human beings, from conception to natural death. By its nature, the Eucharist commits us to the poor and those who are most vulnerable (see CCC, no. 1397).

✠ To make visible the connection between the Eucharist and justice, host a ministry fair after all Sunday Masses for all parish and diocesan ministries that promote the life and dignity of all people. "Our communities, when they celebrate the Eucharist, must become ever more conscious that the sacrifice of Christ is for all, and that the Eucharist thus compels all who believe in him to become 'bread that is broken' for others, and to work for the building of a more just and fraternal world" (Pope Benedict XVI, *The Sacrament of Charity* [*Sacramentum Caritatis*], no. 88).[1]
✠ Provide resources explaining the changes in the Liturgy for those who minister to those who are homebound. Gather these ministers to share ideas about how to ensure that those who cannot attend the Sunday celebration of the Eucharist are incorporated into the parish community.
✠ Prepare homilies or catechetical sessions on the presence of Christ in the Eucharist, the minister, the Word proclaimed, the gathered congregation, and especially the eucharistic species (see SC, no. 7).

November 2011

In November, beginning with **All Saints/All Souls (November 1-2)**, the Church gives special attention to our brothers and sisters who have gone before us in faith. We turn our attention to the communion of saints and to the eschatological nature of the Eucharist:

> Having passed from this world to the Father, Christ gives us in the Eucharist the pledge of glory with him. Participation in the Holy Sacrifice identifies us with his Heart, sustains our strength along the pilgrimage of this life, makes us long for eternal life, and unites us even now to the Church in heaven, the Blessed Virgin Mary, and all the saints. (CCC, no. 1419)

✠ The *Roman Missal* includes many new saints in the liturgical calendar. Invite candidates for Confirmation to research these saints and write short biographies. Publish these biographies in the parish bulletin.
✠ Use Eucharistic Prayer I (the Roman Canon) at Sunday Masses, and mention the saints included in this prayer in the homily.
✠ Consider preaching or hosting a catechetical session on the Eucharist as the wedding feast of the Lamb.

In 2011, **National Bible Week (from Sunday to Sunday of Thanksgiving week)** will begin on the Solemnity of Christ the King and conclude on the First Sunday of Advent, the date of first use of the *Roman Missal*.

✠ Observe National Bible Week with a Bible vigil or Liturgy of the Word with the following theme: "Worship the Father in Spirit and Truth (John 4:23)."
✠ Invite parish youth to participate in a contest for multimedia projects highlighting the biblical roots of the revised Mass texts. Announce the winners during National Bible Week, and display the winning projects in the narthex, in the parish hall, and on the parish Web site.

---

1 See Pope Benedict XVI, *The Sacrament of Charity* (*Sacramentum Caritatis*) (Washington, DC: USCCB, 2007).

✠ Begin publishing the citations for the weekday and Sunday readings in the parish bulletin and on the parish Web site. Encourage parishioners to read each day's readings or to listen to a podcast of daily readings (available at *www.usccb.org/nab/nabpodcast.shtml*).

✠ Find ways to thank all ministers of the Word, including lectors, catechists, and members of the parish evangelization committee.

December 2011

During the **Advent/Christmas season**, beginning with the first Sunday of Advent, parishes across the United States will implement the *Roman Missal*. Because this implementation is a process, not an event, you will want to continue parish catechetical efforts throughout this season.

✠ Have a hot chocolate and cookie social after the Sunday Masses or on a weeknight, as an opportunity for parishioners to ask questions about the changes in the Liturgy.

✠ Send Christmas cards to all registered parishioners, wishing them the joy of the season and inviting them to attend the Eucharistic Liturgy on Christmas and on every Sunday. Make sure you include information about Mass times, the availability of child care, and ministry to those who are homebound. Include a phone number or e-mail address for questions.

✠ Prepare a special bulletin insert or handout about the changes to distribute at the Christmas Masses. Before Christmas, have a special meeting with the ushers and ministers of hospitality to discuss the changes and to prepare them to answer questions from people who may be new to the parish or returning to the practice of the faith.

January 2012

Parishes will have started using the third edition of the *Roman Missal* two months before the observance of **Catholic Schools Week** (beginning the last Sunday in January). However, that does not mean that the catechetical effort has ended. Schools and parishes can use this observance to reinforce the catechetical themes emphasized in the weeks leading up to the implementation.

✠ After the all-school Mass celebrating Catholic Schools Week, host several informal discussions on the Liturgy and the *Roman Missal* with parents, grandparents, and other interested parishioners. You may want to make available some of the catechetical resources used previously, because not all attendees will have received them.

✠ Hold a school-wide contest for essays, posters, or multimedia projects on the theme "Liturgy: Source and Summit of Christian Living." Display the winners in the school during an open house or in the parish narthex and hall after Sunday Masses.

✠ Invite the pastor, principal, teachers, and other adult members of the school community to talk with class groups about how the Eucharistic Liturgy has helped to form their faith.

February and March 2012

During the season of **Lent**, beginning with Ash Wednesday on February 22, 2012, many Catholics return to a fuller practice of their faith. For all of us, it is a time of deeper spiritual reflection and renewal in preparation for the celebration of the Triduum and Easter.

✠ Repeat some or all of the catechetical sessions held during the fall. Announce these sessions in the parish bulletin and on the parish Web site for those who may have missed them.

✠ Pray the liturgical prayers more deliberately, and allow for more silence in the Lenten liturgies, allowing the congregation to reflect more deeply on the words and meaning of the revised prayers.

✠ Include a pastor's column in the parish bulletin discussing worthy reception of the Eucharist. Make sure that the schedule for celebrating the Sacrament of Penance is sufficient, convenient, and well publicized.

April and May 2012

In the season of **Easter**, we join with the neophytes in reflecting on the Paschal Mystery and coming to know Christ more fully "in the breaking of the bread" (Lk 24:35). (Easter is April 8 this year; Pentecost is May 27.)

✠ Prepare a special bulletin insert or handout about the changes in the Mass to distribute at the Easter Masses. Before Easter, have a special meeting with the ushers and ministers of hospitality to discuss the changes and prepare them to answer questions from people who may be new to the parish.

✠ Because many parishes have many new people in attendance on Easter, make it a point to identify and invite these people to come back every Sunday.

✠ Plan a catechetical series on "Catholic basics" for those who may be returning to the practice of the faith. Make the first session about the Eucharistic Liturgy—the source and summit of Christian life.

June 2012

On the feast of the **Body and Blood of Christ (June 10)**, we focus more intently on the Sacrament of the Eucharist. Coming more than six months after the implementation of the *Roman Missal*, this feast is also an opportunity to reflect on the progress the parish has made in implementing the revised texts and renewing its liturgical practice.

✠ Celebrate the Body of Christ with a day of service to the community, followed by Vespers and Benediction. Those unable to participate in the service activities can remain in adoration before the Blessed Sacrament, praying for those who serve and for those who are served.

✠ Because Mass attendance often declines during the summer months, begin a parish campaign using the bulletin, the parish newsletter, the parish Web site, and social media sites to remind people of the importance of the Sunday Liturgy and provide information about how to find Mass times and locations when traveling (*www.masstimes.org*).

✠ Host a special thank-you event for those involved in liturgical ministry. Allow some time during the event to discuss how the implementation has gone, elicit suggestions for the future, and explore questions and answers.

B. SUGGESTIONS FOR PARISHES AND SCHOOLS

The following concrete suggestions will help you implement the vision, goals, and objectives that you have developed for use in your parish or school. The suggestions are organized into five groups according to the areas in which they could be used: general catechesis, training, specific ministry areas, committees, and volunteers. We offer them as starting points for your own creativity and encourage you to adapt them to the needs of your parish or school.

You will find materials—print resources, PDFs, audio, and video—to support many of these suggestions at the following places:

✠ The official Web site of the implementation of the *Roman Missal*, *www.usccb.org/romanmissal*

✠ Appendices B-D for reproducible resources

✠ Appendix F: Resources from Other Publishers and National Organizations for resources available from partner publishers

1. For General Catechesis

The following are ideas about how to share information about the *Roman Missal* and your parish's or school's implementation activities with a broad or mixed group of people.

In the Parish

✠ Feature a quote from the newly translated Mass, accompanied by the bishop's or pastor's reflection on the quote, in the parish bulletin, on the parish Web site, or in parish e-mails.

- Start a weekly or biweekly e-mail newsletter that focuses on an issue or question related to the revised translation. Use the *Roman Missal* Web site (*www. usccb.org/romanmissal*) as a resource for content.
- Include copies of bulletin inserts on the *Roman Missal* in your parish bulletin, starting at least three months before the implementation date. Downloadable, print-ready inserts are available at *www.usccb.org/romanmissal*.
- Post a link to the USCCB's *Roman Missal* Web site (*www.usccb.org/romanmissal*) on the parish's home page. Include or embed links to audio or video relevant to the newly translated texts.
- Invite parishioners to follow or "friend" your parish social networking profile (e.g., Facebook, MySpace, Twitter). Use the profile to post frequent announcements of activities related to the implementation of the *Roman Missal* in the parish.

In the School

- Post a link to the USCCB's *Roman Missal* Web site (*www.usccb.org/romanmissal*) on the school's home page.
- Send parents a letter outlining the schedule of how the implementation will take place in the school setting. Invite parents to contact you with questions or concerns. Host a parent meeting to address common questions.

2. For Training

Liturgical and catechetical ministers in the parish or school setting will need some training to help them effectively implement the changes, especially in the Order of Mass.

In the Parish

- Create a calendar of the many liturgical ministry training opportunities that will be available at the diocesan, regional, and national levels. See Appendix F for a list of organizations and publishers who have scheduled workshops, seminars, or conference sessions for training liturgical ministers.

- Identify online training or learning opportunities for liturgical ministers, including those from publishers and organizations listed in Appendix F and at the *Roman Missal* Web site (*www.usccb. org/romanmissal*). Maintain a list at the liturgy or music ministry pages of the parish Web site. Update it with comments and recommendations from those who attend.
- Send individual liturgical ministers to diocesan or national training sessions (e.g., by the Federation of Diocesan Liturgical Commissions [FDLC]), and then invite them to share what they learned from the experience with a small group of volunteers.
- Host a training session for all extraordinary ministers of the Eucharist—including those who do home, hospital, and prison visits—to go over changes in the prayers. Also, provide them with print or online resources so that they can answer any questions about the changes that may arise during their visits.
- Schedule a training session on liturgy planning for all youth ministry leaders, especially those planning Mass for retreats. Review and discuss the changes in the translation. Talk about how to introduce the changes to the youth and how to help the youth become comfortable with the wording. Spend time reflecting on the revised translations of the Eucharistic Prayers and Prefaces, especially if the group is planning for specific dates. Provide the youth with print resources and links to online resources about the *Roman Missal* from the parish Web site, the USCCB Web site, other national organizations' sites (e.g., National Association of Pastoral Musicians [NPM] and National Federation for Catholic Youth Ministry [NFCYM]), and the sites of liturgical publishers.
- Encourage ushers and ministers of hospitality to indicate the page in the hymnal or music edition where the musical setting for the newly translated eucharistic acclamations can be found.
- Include a Bible-study component in your catechist training session to focus on the Scripture passages underlying the newly translated texts.

In the School

✠ Send religion teachers or campus, youth, or music ministers to diocesan or national training sessions (e.g., by FDLC and NFCYM), and then invite them to share what they learned with their departments and the full staff.

✠ Schedule a training session on liturgy planning for all staff and campus ministry leaders, especially those planning school or retreat Masses. Review and discuss the changes in the translation. Talk about how to introduce them to the youth and how to make youth comfortable with the wordings. Spend time reflecting on the revised translations of the Eucharistic Prayers and Prefaces, especially if the group is planning for specific dates.

✠ Have the pastor or liturgy director address a meeting of the PTA/PTO or home-school association about the changes in the translation. Allow plenty of time for questions. Provide the parents with print resources and links to online resources they can use to help their children prepare for the revised translation. Resources could be made available on the parish Web site; you might also provide links to resources on the USCCB Web site, other national organizations' sites (e.g., NPM, NFCYM), and the sites of liturgical publishers.

3. For Primary Ministry Areas

The following suggestions are for the primary leaders on a parish or school staff (full- or part-time; paid or volunteer), starting with the priest/pastor, who works with other staff or volunteers in a specific ministry area. The parish and school ideas are subdivided into specific ministry or functional areas. Note that some ideas may be duplicated in multiple ministry areas.

Priests/Pastors

✠ Review the backgrounders on the revised translation at the *Roman Missal* Web site (*www.usccb. org/romanmissal*). Summarize the information into short statements (fifty to one hundred words each) so that you have a ready response to questions that parishioners are most likely to ask.

✠ Adapt the responses in the "Questions About the New *Roman Missal*" bulletin insert so that you can easily address your parishioners' concerns in language that is comfortable and familiar to you. The bulletin insert text can be found in this guide; an electronic copy is also available at *www.usccb.org/romanmissal*.

✠ Schedule a "conversation with the pastor"—or a series of them—after the last Mass on a Sunday two to three months before the implementation date. During the session(s), you can help attendees look at the upcoming changes in greater depth in an informal setting.

✠ Invite local experts in worship, translation, or Scripture scholarship to meet and share their insights with the pastors in your own and adjacent parishes, as a part of a regular reflection on the changes.

✠ Use (or create) your pastor's column—in the parish bulletin, at the parish Web site, or in regular parish e-mails—to focus on the revised translation. Address the history of the translation, the relationship of the newly translated texts to Scripture, and the additions made because of the canonization of new saints since the last translation.

✠ Identify opportunities in the Lectionary to preach on or make connections to the newly translated texts. See the *Roman Missal* Web site (*www.usccb. org/romanmissal*) for detailed resources on the scriptural roots of the revised translation.

✠ Compare the existing and newly translated celebrant's texts side by side, and note the specific language that has changed. Listen to the audio resources at the *Roman Missal* Web site (*www. usccb.org/romanmissal*) to familiarize yourself with the rhythm and syntax of the revised wording. Speak the text aloud to identify those texts in which the syntax and wording are challenging. Give special attention to practicing those passages.

✠ Use a blog or a microblogging account (e.g., Twitter) to share your occasional reflections on the translation of the Mass in an informal way. Recommend to your parishioners any television or radio programs or excerpts from books, magazines, or other periodicals that might give them further insight into the changes.

✠ Give engaged couples a printed or download-able copy of the changes to the Mass and an explanation of the changes when they come for their initial meeting or for marriage preparation classes. Review the changes with them, and help them decide how they will make the Order of Mass and people's responses available to those who attend their wedding. For example, will they use the parish's participation aids or hymnals, or might they include the people's responses in their worship aid?

✠ Attend workshops offered by your diocese, FDLC, the National Organization for Continuing Education of Roman Catholic Clergy (NOCERCC), or other national organizations. Share your notes and insights with your staff.

✠ Schedule times during the first six months of the implementation to meet regularly with the pastors in neighboring parishes to share ideas and assess how well the implementation is going.

Parish Leaders and Staff

Liturgy and Music

✠ Attend workshops on the newly translated texts. Workshops may be offered by your diocese, FDLC, NPM, NFCYM, the National Conference for Catechetical Leadership (NCCL), or other national organizations.

✠ Meet initially with the directors of liturgy and music in your local area to compare implementation plans, identify any opportunities to bring your parishes' staffs or volunteers together, and note where and how your plans may differ.

✠ Schedule times during the first six months of the implementation to meet regularly with the directors of liturgy and music in neighboring parishes to check in and see how well the implementation is going. Share success stories, identify best practices, and strategize about how to resolve issues as they emerge.

✠ Identify what print resource(s) you will use to provide the text of the revised translation. Check to see how your worship aid publisher will be implementing the changes. Will the publisher provide a separate print resource of the revised Order of Mass? Will the changes be fully incorporated into the print issue?

✠ Working with your director of religious education or faith formation, decide how liturgy and music staff can help support the implementation of the revised translation during sacramental preparation—such as by practicing the musical setting of the eucharistic acclamations with parents and children.

✠ Again working with your director of religious education or faith formation, determine how the changes will be introduced to the congregation at Sunday Mass. Decide who will lead the instruction, when the instruction will take place, when instruction will start and end, and what will be practiced when.

✠ Review the musical settings of the Mass that the parish uses on a regular basis. Determine how and when you will introduce the changes to the choir, cantors, celebrants, and people. Identify any additional resources (such as audiovisual aids and printed materials) that you will need in addition to the participation aid or hymnal in use.

✠ In an e-mail to all musicians, cantors, and choir members, send Web links to MP3s of music or graphic files of sheet music of Mass settings that will be used in the parish. Post the links on your parish Web site as well, if permitted by the copyright holder. Sources for music files include the publishers, artists themselves, and aggregators like iTunes.

✠ Promote the revised Mass setting to be used at the parish on the parish Web site. With appropriate copyright permission, post a link to audio files so that parishioners can listen and sing along.

✠ Give a printed or downloadable copy of the changes to the Mass, and an explanation of the changes, to engaged couples when they come to plan their weddings.

✠ Let newly engaged couples know what resources the parish has available to help wedding attendees follow and participate in the Mass. Options can include using the parish's participation aids or hymnals or incorporating the people's responses in their worship aid.

- Equip extraordinary ministers of the Eucharist, especially those who do home and hospital visits, with revised ritual books.
- Reflect on Collects and Prefaces of the day or week as part of opening prayer for committee meetings.
- Compare the existing and newly translated texts side by side, and note the specific language that has changed.
- Identify how the translation will affect the liturgical ministers and what additional training they will need to help ease the transition, especially with sung texts.

Religious Education

- Talk with your religion textbook sales representative as soon as possible to a year before the implementation starts, to find out how the publisher will be handling the text revisions, how it will make sure you have the right quantity of the right version, and how it will handle returns of the unrevised editions.
- Find out what online resources your textbook publisher will make available to support the transition to the revised texts.
- Take a tour of the Web site of your textbook publisher with all catechists to review what resources will be available now and in the future to help with the implementation.
- Meet initially with the directors of religious education in your local area to compare your implementation plans, identify any opportunities to bring your parishes' staffs or volunteers together, and note where and how your plans may differ.
- Schedule times during the first six months of the implementation to meet regularly with the directors of religious education in neighboring parishes to check in and see how well the implementation is going. Share success stories, identify best practices, and strategize about how to resolve issues as they emerge.
- Decide how the revised translation will be introduced in sacramental preparation programs. Consider reviewing the Mass and the people's parts during preparation for Reconciliation and Confirmation as well as First Communion, highlighting these sacraments' relationships to the Eucharist.

- Working with your liturgy director and music director, determine how the changes will be introduced to the congregation at Sunday Mass. Decide who will lead the instruction, when the instruction will take place, when instruction will start and end, and what will be practiced when.
- Meet with your liturgy director and music director to identify how they can help support the introduction of the *Roman Missal* during your sacramental preparation programs.
- Include a Bible-study component in your catechist training session to focus on the Scripture passages that underlie the newly translated texts.
- Make "Scripture and the Eucharist," or "Scripture and the Mass," the theme of your vacation Bible school. Structure sessions around Bible searches and discussions of the Scripture passages that form the foundations for the texts of the Mass, especially the newly translated ones. Make this an opportunity for children to rediscover the essential relationship between Scripture and Mass and to practice their parts in the Mass.
- Develop a one-page explanation of the relationship between the Eucharist and each of the other sacraments celebrated in the parish. Distribute this along with a print copy of the revised translation of the Mass to all catechists, volunteers, and parents.
- Attend workshops on the newly translated texts. Workshops may be offered by your diocese, FDLC, NPM, NCCL, NFCYM, or other national organizations.
- Reflect on Collects and Prefaces of the day or week as part of opening prayer for committee meetings.

Adult Faith Formation

- Host a multiweek Bible study focusing on the Scripture passages that underlie the newly translated texts.
- Schedule three extended or short series of adult faith formation sessions to study the revised translation. Host one session before the implementation, another session within the first two months, and the last session three to six months after the implementation. Explore the historical

roots of the texts, the process of translation and its evolution, and topics related to rhythm and speaking in unison.

✠ Focus your parish mission on the Eucharist and how the words of the Mass form us in our faith.

✠ Reflect on Collects and Prefaces of the day or week as part of opening prayer for committee meetings.

RCIA and Evangelization

✠ Review the materials used in your RCIA program that relate to the Mass. Identify what you will replace them with or what supplements you will add to provide the appropriate information about the newly translated texts.

✠ Meet initially with the directors of RCIA and evangelization in your local area to compare your implementation plans, identify any opportunities to bring your parishes' staffs or volunteers together, and note where and how your plans may differ.

✠ Schedule times during the first six months of the implementation to meet regularly with the directors of RCIA and evangelization in neighboring parishes to check in and see how well the implementation is going. Share success stories, identify best practices, and strategize about how to help resolve issues as they emerge.

✠ Provide catechumens and candidates with a side-by-side comparison of the people's parts, an explanation of the changes, and an explanation of the history of translation in the Catholic Tradition.

✠ Invite the pastor or a local Catholic scholar to share reflections on translation in the Catholic Tradition with the catechumens and candidates.

✠ Encourage small Christian communities, faith-sharing groups, and prayer groups to focus a series of meetings on the revised translation of the Mass. Direct them to resources such as those available at the *Roman Missal* Web site (*www.usccb.org/romanmissal*) and in Appendix D of this guide.

✠ Make the implementation of the revised translation an opportunity to invite inactive Catholics back to the Church and to participation in the sacraments. Sponsor an evening or weekend session, or series of sessions, to discuss the Sacrament of the Eucharist, the Mass, and the changes to the Mass.

✠ Develop a direct mail, phone, or e-mail campaign to invite all parishioners to Mass during the early months of the implementation. Use this as an opportunity to reach out to parishioners, remind them of your Mass schedule, and promote other services, such as babysitting, young family programs, or adult faith formation programs.

✠ Reflect on Collects and Prefaces of the day or week as part of opening prayer for committee meetings.

Youth and Young Adult Ministry

✠ Meet initially with the directors of youth and young adult ministry in your local area to compare your implementation plans, identify any opportunities to bring your parishes' staffs or volunteers together, and note where and how your plans may differ.

✠ Schedule times during the first six months of the implementation to meet regularly with the directors of youth and young adult ministry in neighboring parishes to check in and see how well the implementation is going. Share success stories, identify best practices, and strategize about how to help resolve issues as they emerge.

✠ Host a biweekly or monthly Bible study that focuses on the Scripture passages that underlie the newly translated texts. Invite youth leaders to prepare for and lead these sessions.

✠ Host youth group sessions on the Mass, inviting youth leaders to prepare and lead the sessions.

✠ Attend workshops on the newly translated texts offered by your diocese, FDLC, NPM, NCCL, NFCYM, or other national organizations.

✠ Reflect on Collects and Prefaces of the day or week as part of opening prayer for committee meetings.

Other Ministries and Parish Secretary

✠ Order copies of the *Roman Missal* for each worship site, celebrant, and any other key staff people.

✠ Let newly engaged couples know if the parish has any particular resources available to help wedding attendees follow and participate in the

Mass. Options can include using the parish's participation aids or hymnals or incorporating the people's responses in their worship aid.

✠ Work with the chaplains of the local hospitals, nursing homes, and prisons or jails to identify what materials they will need and are allowed to distribute to help residents learn the people's parts and to answer any questions they have.

✠ Purchase or create bookmarks to mark the starting page of the musical setting for all funeral Masses.

✠ Schedule your staff retreat for six to twelve months before the implementation date. Use the time to prayerfully create your parish implementation plan and to reflect on and celebrate the Eucharist together.

✠ Reflect on Collects and Prefaces of the day or week as part of opening prayer for staff meetings.

School Leaders and Staff

Principals and Administration

✠ Ensure that religion teachers have set aside specific sessions to review and practice the people's parts, especially in the months prior to the implementation.

✠ Invite a local member of a national Catholic ministry organization (see the list Appendix F) or diocesan staff person to speak at your staff meeting about how the changes in the Mass will affect the children and young people, what questions to expect, and how to address them.

✠ Reflect on Collects and Prefaces of the day/week as part of opening prayer for staff meetings.

Teachers

✠ Talk with your religion textbook sales representative as soon as possible to a year before the implementation, to find out how the publisher will be handling the text revisions, how it will make sure you have the right quantity of the right version, and how it will handle returns of the unrevised editions.

✠ Find out what online resources your textbook publisher will make available to support the transition to the revised texts.

✠ Take a tour of your textbook publisher's Web site with all religion teachers to review what resources will be available now and in the future to help with the implementation.

✠ Review sacramental preparation texts to ensure that the school has sufficient copies of the revised editions.

✠ Set aside specific class sessions to review and practice the people's parts, especially in the months prior to the implementation.

✠ Attend workshops on the *Roman Missal*. Workshops may be offered by your diocese, the National Catholic Educational Association (NCEA), NCCL, NFCYM, or other national organizations.

✠ Invite a local member of a national Catholic ministry organization (see the list in Appendix F) or diocesan staff person to speak at your staff meeting about how the changes in the Mass will affect the children and young people, what questions to expect, and how to address them.

✠ Create a Bible scavenger hunt in which students match up the newly translated text with its scriptural roots.

✠ In language classes, compare the newly translated English Mass texts to those in the language being learned to identify the similarities and differences. For example, highlight the fact that the phrase "And with your spirit"—a change in the English translation—has been the norm in many other languages, including Spanish and French, since the Liturgy was first translated into vernacular languages.

✠ Reflect on Collects and Prefaces of the day or week as part of opening prayer for departmental meetings and at the beginning of class periods.

Campus Ministry (High School)

✠ Practice the people's responses over the public address system the day before the first school Mass in which the revised texts will be used. Provide hard copies of the people's responses for students to take home and practice further with their parents.

- ✠ Attend workshops offered by your diocese, NPM, NCEA, NCCL, NFCYM, or other national organizations.
- ✠ Reflect on Collects and Prefaces of the day or week as part of opening prayer for staff meetings.
- ✠ Order copies of the *Roman Missal* for each worship site, celebrant, campus minister, and key staff person.

Campus Ministry (College)

- ✠ Make extra copies of the people's parts available in the church/chapel and lobby areas for students to take with them.
- ✠ Include a link to the *Roman Missal* Web site (*www.usccb.org/romanmissal*) on your Web page.
- ✠ Work with student leaders to develop age-appropriate reflections on the newly translated Collects and Prefaces. Publish these on your Web page, through a blog, or in an audio or video podcast.
- ✠ Work with retreat leaders to develop a brief catechetical session to introduce and practice the newly translated texts on retreats where Mass is celebrated.
- ✠ Have copies of church documents on the Mass and Eucharist (see the list of key documents in Part III for suggested titles) available to lend to students.
- ✠ Encourage small groups or small faith-sharing communities to reflect on the newly translated texts as part of their regular meetings, especially during the eight- to ten-week period before the date of first use.
- ✠ Attend workshops offered by your diocese, NPM, NCEA, NCCL, the National Association of Diocesan Directors of Campus Ministry (NADDCM), the Catholic Campus Ministry Association (CCMA), or other national organizations.
- ✠ Reflect on Collects and Prefaces of the day or week as part of opening prayer for staff meetings.
- ✠ Order copies of the *Roman Missal* for each worship site, celebrant, campus minister, and key staff person.

4. For Volunteers

In the Parish

- ✠ Invite a locally or nationally known liturgical composer to lead an evening of reflection and music for your parish volunteers. Invite other area parishes to co-sponsor the event.
- ✠ Host an informal session of all extraordinary ministers of the Eucharist, especially those who make home, hospital, and prison visits. At the session, discuss and practice how to respond to questions about the changes in the translation.

In the School

- ✠ Distribute copies of the side-by-side comparison of the translations of the people's parts to parents at a PTA/PTO meeting two to three months before implementation. Include copies in your parents' newsletter.
- ✠ Invite the pastor, or the parish or diocesan liturgy director, to lead a question-and-answer session on the changes in the Mass at a PTA/PTO meeting.

PART III

AN IN-DEPTH IMPLEMENTATION PROCESS

Part I gave a general overview of the planning process, including a focused approach that can be followed by parishes and schools with limited resources. Part II provided a timeline and suggested specific activities that parishes and schools might wish to follow.

Part III provides a detailed implementation process for parishes and schools with the interest, time, and resources to target a deeper renewal of the community's liturgical life. Sections A and B are directed to the parish or school leader who has the overall responsibility for implementation of the *Roman Missal*. These sections outline the intended outcomes of the process and provide information on identifying the planning team including who the facilitator will be. Sections C and D are specifically directed toward the facilitator. Section C should be used at the first planning team meeting to set the groundwork for the parish or school's implementation process.

A. PREPARATORY STEPS

1. Outcomes and Definitions

Outcomes

This process has three outcomes:

1. To set a strategic vision for the implementation based on your parish's mission
2. To identify what you want to achieve (goals and objectives) as a result of the implementation of the *Roman Missal*
3. To develop an Action Plan that will help you achieve your goals and objectives

Definitions

Strategic Vision
A **strategic vision** deals with the mission and direction that the parish wishes to embrace as it prepares to implement the *Roman Missal*. It sketches out the desired big-picture impact. The strategic vision statement tells the story of *what* the parish hopes to accomplish and *why* this work is important.

Goals

Goals elaborate on the *what* and describe in greater detail specific "destination points" on the way to accomplishing the parish's mission and vision. Goals are the bridge between the big picture of the strategic vision and the small picture of the objectives. Work on goals may be shared by staff and committees who have responsibility for specific objectives related to the goal.

Objectives

Objectives continue to refine the response to the question *what* to accomplish and are specifically related to individual goals. Objectives are concrete and measurable. They describe *how* to accomplish the goal.

Action Plan

The **Action Plan** includes concrete activities and tasks, a timeline for implementation, a list of who is responsible for what, and a list of what resources are needed for the activities. It also prioritizes the activities so that resources are used as effectively as possible. The Action Plan is the blueprint or road map that a parish uses to accomplish the goals and objectives and achieve its mission and vision.

2. Identifying the Planning Team

Part I's discussion on the ABCs of planning noted that the key to any successful pastoral strategy or ministry is the people who are involved. Therefore, as your parish or school community begins its planning, identify the key people who should be involved, and secure their participation. Invite people from a broad cross-section of ministries and ministers, volunteer and paid.

Decision Making

Take time to clarify who has decision-making responsibilities and how decisions will be made, both for the parish and for specific ministries. For example, will the parish staff decide which resources the parish should use to support the implementation—e.g., hymnals and catechetical resources—or will the planning team make that decision? Ensure that the facilitator understands who has decision-making responsibilities and how decisions will be made, so that he or she can clearly articulate that to the planning team.

Facilitator

Choose one person to be the lead coordinator or facilitator for the planning team. This person is not necessarily the decision maker; rather, he or she will be charged with staying on top of the various planning activities. Send the facilitator a complete contact list of the planning team members and the roles and responsibilities chart below.

The following is a list of general responsibilities of the facilitator.

- Lead all planning team meetings, especially the facilitated implementation planning process that begins in Section B.
- Coordinate the time and place of the planning team meetings.
- Prepare an opening and closing prayer.
- Coordinate set-up of the space, including all materials needed.
- Explain the purpose, format, and structure of each meeting.
- Establish small groups, if needed, and designate a small-group leader or reporter.
- If appropriate, address questions, comments, or insights from previous meetings.
- Facilitate large-group discussion questions or sharing summaries of small-group conversations.
- Close each meeting with a summary of the conclusions and decisions that have been made.
- Prepare and lead the meeting evaluation.
- Summarize meeting evaluations, and produce a report for the parish or school leadership.

Planning Team Members

Worksheet 1—Roles and Responsibilities is an outline of the key people for the planning. (A modifi-
able and downloadable electronic version of Worksheet 1 can be found at *www.usccb.org/romanmissal*.)
Add to and modify the responsibilities listed in
Worksheet 1 so that they reflect the skills and experiences of your parish leaders. Consider the following question: what other ministries or committees
should be invited that are not listed here? Add these
and their related responsibilities in the appropriate
areas of Worksheet 1.

Invite your potential team members personally, and follow up with a letter or e-mail that
includes Worksheet 1 and the date, time, and place
of the first team meeting. (Use the downloadable,
electronic version of Worksheet 1 to create smaller
charts, or send it as an e-mail attachment.) Review
the roles and responsibilities of each person on the
planning team. Once all team members have confirmed their participation, consider posting a version
of the chart at your parish or school Web site as part
of your strategy for communicating with with the
parish or school community.

3. Materials Needed and Preparatory Steps

Materials

✠ Copies of each of the following, one per participant:
  • Parish or school mission statement (see sidebar)
  • Worksheet 1—Roles and Responsibilities
  • Worksheet 2—Personal Expectations
  • Worksheet 3—Creating a Strategic Vision
    Statement
  • Worksheet 4—Developing Goals and Objectives
  • Worksheet 6—Twelve-Month Planning Calendar
  • Handout 1—Key Documents
  • Handout 2—Opening and Closing Prayers
  • Handout 3—Components of a Strategic Vision
    Statement
  • Evaluation
✠ Multiple copies of Worksheet 5—Action Plan
  by Objective

✠ Pens or pencils—one per participant
✠ Newsprint and markers
✠ Masking tape
✠ Nametags
✠ One copy of each of the following documents
  for reference
  • *Constitution on the Sacred Liturgy* (*Sacrosanc-
    tum Concilium*)
  • *General Instruction of the Roman Missal*

> If your parish or school does not have a
> mission statement, there is a short process
> for developing one in Session 1.

Preparation

✠ Confirm the start and end times for the session.
✠ Determine when to arrive in order to set up the
  site. Let whomever is in charge of the space know
  how you want the chairs arranged.
✠ Identify who will be responsible for refreshments,
  what refreshments will be available, and where
  they will be set up.
✠ Make copies of all worksheets and handouts
  listed above.
✠ Study the revised text and key documents.
  • Visit *www.usccb.org/romanmissal* to review the
    newly translated text of the *Roman Missal*.
  • Review the significant sections of the key
    documents in Handout 1—Key Documents.
    Identify specific sections or paragraphs of the
    key documents on Handout 1 that participants
    should read in preparation for the meeting.
✠ Send a follow-up mailing to the planning team
  that introduces you as the facilitator; reminds
  them of the date, time, and place of the planning
  team meeting; and includes a copy of Worksheet
  2—Personal Expectations and Handout 1—Key
  Documents. Ask them to read Worksheet 2 and
  respond to the reflection questions before coming
  to the first meeting. Recommend specific para-
  graphs or sections in the key documents listed in
  Handout 1 to focus their reading.
✠ Plan an opening and closing prayer.

- Be sure to begin and end the prayer with the Sign of the Cross.
- Include a reading from Sacred Scripture and time for reflection for each prayer. Consider choosing a Scripture citation from those referenced in Handout 1—Key Documents.
- Use the prayers in Handout 2—Opening and Closing Prayers after the Scripture reading and reflection to end the prayer.
- Invite team members to lead the prayer or proclaim the reading. Give readers the citation so they can locate a copy of the reading in advance.

✠ Identify any ground rules that will support good communication for use during the session: e.g., "one person speaks at a time"; "all perspectives are welcome." Consider writing the rules on a piece of newsprint and posting it in the room where it is visible during the team meeting.

✠ If there will be eight or more participants, consider dividing the participants into small groups of three to five for discussion. This may be done before the meeting or during the introduction section. Ask one person in each group to take notes and report back to the large group during the discussions.

✠ Develop an oral or written meeting evaluation that addresses the following questions. Adapt the questions to fit the specific needs of your team.
- Include questions concerning the structure and format.
    ✦ Could the facilitator and any other leaders be seen and heard?
    ✦ Was the room set-up helpful in promoting active participation and discussion?
    ✦ Were the preparatory materials helpful?
- Include questions concerning the session.
    ✦ Were the team members' expectations of the meeting met? Why? Why not?
    ✦ What aspect of the meeting energized them?
    ✦ What did participants take away from the meeting?
    ✦ What did they find helpful? Not helpful?
- Include questions to determine what follow-up needs to take place.
    ✦ What can the parish or school do to support further discussion and reflection on the implementation of the *Roman Missal*, Third Edition?

    ✦ How can the parish or school best communicate the results of the work that was done at this meeting?
    ✦ Who else needs to be engaged in the implementation who is not here or not represented at this meeting?

✠ Arrive early to confirm that the room is set up properly, the newsprint with markers is positioned where everyone can see it, and refreshments are available. Place a pen or pencil and copies of all worksheets and handouts at team members' seats before they arrive.

✠ As people arrive, greet them, invite them to create a name tag, and direct them to refreshments, if available.

B. FACILITATED IMPLEMENTATION PLANNING PROCESS

Use the following session as the agenda for one of your team's first meetings. Two schedule options are listed below. Option 1 outlines a one-session process that takes 2 ½ to 3 hours that could be held in an evening or on a weekend morning or afternoon. Option 2 outlines a two-session process that takes about 2 hours per session; it could be held on two evenings or could cover a full day.

Schedule

Option 1

✠ Welcome (5-10 minutes)
✠ Opening Prayer (5-10 minutes)
✠ Introduction (10-15 minutes)
✠ Session 1: Developing a Strategic Vision Statement (40-45 minutes)
✠ Break (5-10 minutes)
✠ Session 2: Developing Goals and Objectives (30-35 minutes)
✠ Session 3: Creating an Action Plan (30-35 minutes)
✠ Evaluation and Next Steps (10-15 minutes)
✠ Closing Prayer (5-10 minutes)

Option 2

Session 1

✠ Welcome (10-15 minutes)
✠ Opening Prayer (5-10 minutes)
✠ Introduction (10-15 minutes)
✠ Session 1: Developing a Strategic Vision Statement (50-60 minutes)
✠ Next Steps (10-15 minutes)
✠ Closing Prayer (5-10 minutes)

Session 2

✠ Welcome (10-15 minutes)
✠ Opening Prayer (5-10 minutes)
✠ Session 2: Developing Goals and Objectives (35-40 minutes)
✠ Session 3: Creating an Action Plan (35-40 minutes)
✠ Evaluation and Next Steps (10-15 minutes)
✠ Closing Prayer (5-10 minutes)

Welcome

✠ Welcome the team members and give them a verbal tour of the space, including where they might go during the break and where refreshments are.
✠ Introduce yourself as the facilitator. Briefly note what your overall responsibilities are during the meeting.
✠ Invite participants to introduce themselves, especially what ministries they represent. Consider asking them to briefly share a memory of a favorite experience of Mass.
✠ Note that all worksheets and handouts are at their seats. Ask everyone to find Handout 2—Opening and Closing Prayers.

Opening Prayer

✠ Ask the prayer leader to begin.
✠ Readers may read from their places, sitting or standing, depending upon space.

Introduction

✠ Give an overview of the schedule and four primary sessions of the meeting. Note that the work completed at this meeting will be the foundation for the implementation of the *Roman Missal* throughout the parish or school.
✠ Review your ground rules with the team. Note that these principles can guide how the group works—as individuals and as a team—to achieve excellence.
✠ If needed, divide the participants into their small groups. Small groups should be no more than three to five people to give everyone the opportunity to participate equally fully.
✠ Lead the team in a brief conversation about personal expectations. Using their responses on Worksheet 2—Personal Expectations, invite team members share their reflections to each set of question. Note their responses on newsprint and review them, highlighting those that the process will and will not address. Plan to come back to those that the process will not address, and develop specific strategies to deal with them.

Session 1: Developing a Strategic Vision Statement

Context for the Implementation

✠ Present the following points to the team.
  • The implementation of the revised translation takes place within the context of the Catholic Church in the United States, its dioceses, and your parish or school community.
  • The Church's history and Tradition are rich and expansive.
  • Within the larger Church, your parish or school has unique gifts that it nurtures and offers to enrich the larger Catholic community.
  • It is important to identify the unique vision for the implementation that best reflects the Church, her Tradition, and your parish's or school's uniqueness.

✠ Using Handout 1—Key Documents, invite the team members to respond to two questions, noting their responses on newsprint.
- What is the Church's vision for the liturgy as set forth in these documents?
- What does this vision mean for our parish or school today?

✠ Read the parish or school mission statement aloud (see sidebar if your parish or school does not have a mission statement). Ask the team members the following:
- What is the vision for the liturgy that our parish or school mission statement states or suggests?
- What aspects of the Church's vision does it reflect?
- What do we need to add to or change in our parish or school mission statement to better reflect the Church's vision for the liturgy?

If your parish or school does not have a mission statement, lead the team in answering the following questions.

- Who are we as a parish or school?
- What are our values? How do we do things at the parish?
- What do we hope to achieve as a parish or school?

Assessing the Present Reality

✠ In small groups, assess the present reality of your parish or school by responding to the following questions.
- What is happening in the Church and our parish or school that affects our ability to achieve our mission?
- What are the **strengths** of our parish or school community that we want to build on during this implementation?
- What are the **potential opportunities** presented by the implementation that we could take advantage of to build a stronger parish or school liturgical community?

- What are the **weaknesses** of our parish or school community that we want to avoid during this implementation?
- What are the **potential threats** that could derail a successful implementation of the *Roman Missal*?

✠ Reconvene the group, and invite participants to share the answers with the large group. List responses on newsprint. Set these aside for use during the next steps and the session on goals and objectives.

What Is a Strategic Vision Statement?

✠ Share the following with your team about the vision statement.
- A strategic vision statement is about decision making.
  - ✦ It creates consistency and intentionality in the decision-making process.
  - ✦ It helps the parish or school make choices that are conscious.
  - ✦ It requires value-based criteria to guide future decisions.
- A strategic vision statement creates awareness of what is important to the parish or school and how well various options align with the parish's or school's values.
  - ✦ It supports the parish's or school's mission and its advantages.
  - ✦ It ensures that the plans meet financial and quality criteria and address the needs of the intended audience.
  - ✦ It positions the parish or school and its team as leader of the change.

✠ Review Handout 3—Components of a Strategic Vision Statement. Point out that the strategic vision statement is basically a long, complex sentence, consisting of seven components. Explain that the team will be working to fill in the blanks during the rest of the session.

Creating a Parish or School Strategic Vision Statement

Using Worksheet 3—Creating a Strategic Vision Statement, lead the team through the process of drafting a strategic vision statement by filling in the "Parish or School Strategy Statement" column. Once you have completed Worksheet 3, you should be able to read it as a comprehensive strategic vision statement.

Components

Note that each component listed below corresponds to a section on Worksheet 3.

✠ Component 1: Examine the parish or school mission statement.
  • Instruct the team members to write in the parish or school mission statement in the Parish or School Strategy Statement column.
  • Ask team members to specify any aspects of or implications of the mission statement on the liturgical and catechetical life of the parish or school.

✠ Component 2: What do you seek to accomplish through this implementation strategy—beyond becoming familiar with the revised rite? Brainstorm answers to this question. Refer to newsprint from the team's work on assessing the present reality for ideas on how to build on strengths, address weaknesses, take advantage of new opportunities, and minimize potential threats.

✠ Component 3: Identify all of the groups of people that the parish or school serves. Group those by like ministries or related ministries. Note which people are leaders.

✠ Component 4: Name your key collaborators and stakeholders—those who will affect and be affected by the implementation of the *Roman Missal*. These people might include diocesan and parish or school leaders, parents, key suppliers, even local community organizations.

✠ Component 5: List the key activities and responsibilities of the parish or school that help you work toward your mission and vision.

✠ Component 6: Describe your parish's or school's "comparative advantage." Comparative advantage includes the unique aspects of the parish or school that distinguish it from other parishes or schools, especially when it comes to making a change. It is the ability to have an impact, make a difference, or fulfill a mission. It is the sum of your parish's or school's strengths, gifts, and resources—all the positive qualities you bring to the table.
  • Which of the strengths that we already named give us a comparative advantage for this implementation?
  • What other gifts and resources will help us make this implementation a transformative experience for the parish or school?
  • What do we do best?

✠ Component 7: Core values are beliefs that sustain your work and mission, the parish or school's culture, and your staff. They are what you hold to as you build and support your parish or school's identity. Name your parish's core values, especially those that you need to pay close attention to during the implementation.

Finalizing the Strategic Vision Statement

✠ Read through the strategic vision statement developed in Worksheet 3. Discuss any questions, concerns, or insights as a team.

✠ Identify any changes that could be made. With the general consensus of the team, incorporate them into the vision statement.

✠ Based on the strategic vision statement, ask the group to identify the criteria that you will use to decide what goals, objectives, and activities you will implement for the *Roman Missal*. Highlight the top five or six criteria. List these criteria on a piece of newsprint, and post it where everyone can see it. These will be used later in Session 3, the Action Plan session.

Break

Session 2: Developing Goals and Objectives

✠ Review Goals 1 and 2 on Worksheet 4—Developing Goals and Objectives. These are the two goals for the implementation of the *Roman Missal* that are also featured in Part I of this *Leader's Guide*. They form the core of and starting point for your parish or school goal-setting process.

✠ Identify and discuss other goals that you might want to pursue as part of the implementation. Other goals might focus on specific pastoral areas, such as
  • Outreach to and welcoming of inactive Catholics in your area
  • Support for parents as catechists in the home
  • Promotion of the relationship between the Eucharist and justice

✠ Evaluate the proposed goals using the strategic vision statement and your criteria for decision making to determine which goals will help you accomplish your vision. Keep the total number of goals to no more than five. Ask each team member to write the goals down in the space provided on Worksheet 4.

✠ Assign one goal per small group (multiple groups may work on the same goal). If the team is small, divide the team into pairs, and have each pair work on one goal.

✠ Ask each group to identify possible objectives that will help you accomplish its assigned goal. Remind the team that objectives should be concrete and measurable—anyone should be able to recognize when an objective has been completed.

✠ The groups that are working with goals 1 and 2 should start by reviewing the objectives listed on Worksheet 4 and checking off those that your parish or school may wish to pursue. Encourage the group to identify additional objectives for goals 1 and 2 that are not on this list, especially ones that address specific needs or take advantage of your parish's or school's particular strengths and gifts.

✠ Gather everyone back into the large group. Ask each small group to share the objectives it identified. Invite the team to add or clarify any of the objectives.

✠ Have the same small groups reconvene and prioritize their objectives. Encourage them to use the vision statement and criteria as they evaluate the objectives. Then ask them to identify how you will measure the successful completion of each objective. For example, "success" might be defined as completing two training sessions or posting the parish Action Plan on your Web site.

IMPORTANT NOTE

In identifying objectives, it may be easy to overlook communications. Make sure that one of your stated objectives is to communicate your vision and goals to the parish. Identify the messages that you want to convey about the *Roman Missal* and determine how you will communicate those messages—e.g., by Web site, in the parish bulletin, and through parish announcements. Draw on the expertise of parishioners who work in communications, marketing, and advertising. Ask for their input, and invite their participation in this important objective.

Session 3: Creating an Action Plan

✠ Lead a discussion based on the following questions. Note the group's responses on newsprint.
  • What currently planned activities can be used to assist in the implementation?
  • What resources are available to us—staff, volunteers, facilities, funds, and time?

✠ Divide into the same small groups as before, and distribute multiple copies of Worksheet 5—Action Plan by Objective to each small group. Also provide each group with multiple sheets of newsprint and a marker.

✠ Ask the team members to identify the following for each objective, and list this information on newsprint. Remind the small groups to use the values and criteria that they established in the strategic vision statement to help guide your decisions.

- Ways to measure the completion or success of the objective (i.e., how will you know you have accomplished what you set out to do?)
- Activities that will help the parish or school achieve each objective
- Schedule or timeline for each activity, including start and end dates
- Resources needed to implement the activity (e.g., people, budget, materials)
- Who will take responsibility for each activity
- The priority of each activity that is listed

✠ Post the newsprint from each small group around the room.

✠ Invite everyone to walk around the room and read the work of each small group. Ask them to make notes for themselves on the following questions.
- What could work well?
- What do you have concerns about?
- What have we overlooked?
- Where do our needs potentially exceed our available resources, including personnel?
- Where are there overlaps?
- Where are there contradictions? (For example, is a similar activity given a high priority and low priority in two different goals?)

✠ Lead a discussion based on the above questions. Add to, delete, and change the lists of objectives and activities based on the conversation. If activities or issues arise that require more time and attention, you might handle this situation in one of the following ways:
- Ask the small group responsible for that goal if they could meet outside this meeting to do that work.
- Ask the parish or school staff if they could address this at one of their upcoming meetings.
- Ask if a small group of planning team members would like to meet to work on these activities and issues.

✠ Test the timeline for the activities by completing Worksheet 6—Twelve-Month Planning Calendar as a large group. To keep this step brief, abbreviate the goals, objectives, and activities as needed.

✠ Review the timeline. Identify time periods when multiple activities will be happening and resources could be stretched. Come up with strategies to ensure that people and resources are available, or negotiate a change in the timeline within the larger plan for those activities.

✠ Gauge support for the overall plan at this time by inviting the team's responses to these three questions. Note the number of people who raise their hands for each.
- Who can support the overall plan with no reservations?
- Who can support the plan with some reservations?
- Who cannot support the plan?

✠ Starting with those who cannot support the plan, ask them to name their concerns. With the group, identify whether this concern can be addressed in the context of this meeting or whether it needs to be addressed at another time and, possibly, with other people present. Ask the team members who cannot support the plan whether they would be able to do so if their concerns were addressed.

✠ Find out what reservations team members have, and invite the group to try to address or resolve them. Ask these team members if they can support the plan at this point.

✠ If some team members are unable to support it or still have reservations, identify to whom they can address their concerns, and describe how their concerns will be addressed. Make sure that someone from the planning team or parish or school staff has responsibility for following up on them.

Evaluation and Next Steps

✠ Offer the following questions as a starting point for the evaluation. Takes notes on those responses. Include those in your evaluation to the pastor or the parish or school committee.
- What were your insights?
- How well were your expectations for the meeting met?
- What will we do to follow up on these insights?
- What change could this plan cause in our parish or school?
- What are the important next steps?

✠ Distribute the written evaluation forms. Give participants five minutes to complete the forms.

ALTERNATIVE WAY TO CREATE AN ACTION PLAN

Increasing ownership of the planning and implementation of the *Roman Missal* can make for a smoother transition as well as ensure that the parish or school takes advantage of all potential opportunities. One way to do this is to invite other parish or school groups, including established committees, to plan the action steps for objectives for which they might take some leadership.

- Encourage committees to make this process a significant agenda item for their next meeting.
- Ask members of the planning team to be able to give an overview of the vision, mission, goals, and objectives at committee meetings.
- Have a list for committee chairs of planning team members who would be available to facilitate the meetings and answer questions.
- Suggest that the meeting facilitators use the outline for Session 3, "Creating an Action Plan," as a starting point for the process.

✠ Ask for any verbal feedback that may or may not be covered in the evaluation forms.
✠ Following the session, review the written evaluations and compile a summary of the team members' responses.
✠ Write an evaluation of the session(s) from your perspective. Note any follow-up that needs to take place on concerns or issues related to the planning team's support of the plan.
✠ Deliver the summary to the parish or school leadership.

Closing Prayer

✠ Ask the leader of prayer and musicians, if music is part of the prayer, to come forward and take their places.
✠ Readers may come forward or read from their places, depending upon space.
✠ Invite everyone to gather around the prayer table. If space is tight, ask everyone to stand in their places.
✠ When prayer is finished, invite participants to continue their conversations and enjoy the refreshments, if time allows.

C. WORKSHEETS AND HANDOUTS

This section contains the following planning worksheets and handouts.

✠ Worksheet 1—Roles and Responsibilities
✠ Worksheet 2—Personal Expectations
✠ Worksheet 3—Creating a Strategic Vision Statement
✠ Worksheet 4—Developing Goals and Objectives
✠ Worksheet 5—Action Plan by Objective
✠ Worksheet 6—Twelve-Month Planning Calendar
✠ Handout 1—Key Documents
✠ Handout 2—Opening and Closing Prayers
✠ Handout 3—Components of a Strategic Vision Statement

WORKSHEET 1—ROLES AND RESPONSIBILITIES

PARISH LEADERS

Priest/Pastor

- Provide overall leadership for the parish's implementation.
- Promote catechesis on the revised texts through public preaching, writing, and reflection.
- Support parish leaders as they catechize and train other leaders and parishioners to fully participate in the revised Mass.
- Identify the primary coordinator to facilitate the implementation at the parish or school.
-
-
-

Liturgy Director and Music Director

- Provide liturgical and musical leadership for the parish's implementation.
- Train liturgical ministers on how the *Roman Missal, Third Edition*, affects their ministry.
- Provide and promote implementation resources among volunteers and parishioners.
-
-
-

Director of Religious Education

- Provide catechetical leadership for all age groups for the parish's implementation.
- Train catechists and parents on how to teach children about the revised Mass.
- Provide and promote implementation resources among volunteers and parishioners.
- Coordinate catechetical and educational implementation activities with the school principal.
-
-
-

Youth Ministry Director/Coordinator

- Provide leadership for the parish's implementation, especially in youth ministry.
- Assist with training youth ministry leadership.
- Provide age-appropriate resources to youth.
-
-
-

Parish Staff/Secretary

- Support implementation in various ministry areas.
- Provide administrative and/or program assistance during implementation.
-
-
-

SCHOOL LEADERS

Principal/Campus Ministry Leader

- Provide overall leadership for the implementation in the school or university.
- Provide and promote implementation resources for school leaders, including campus ministers and teachers.
- Coordinate catechetical and educational implementation activities with the director of religious education.
-
-
-

Teachers/Campus Ministers

- Provide specific liturgical and catechetical leadership for the school's or university's implementation through the campus ministry office.
- Train liturgical ministers on how the *Roman Missal* affects their ministry.
- Provide and promote implementation resources to school and student leaders.
- Support teachers and parents with resources on how to teach children, young people, and young adults about the revised Mass.
-
-
-

PARISH COMMITTEES

Parish Council and Finance Council

- Provide leadership and support, including budgeting, for the implementation.
- Provide guidance and feedback to the pastor and parish staff from the parish and other parish committees.
-
-
-

Liturgy and Music

- Support the liturgy director and music director during implementation.
- Provide guidance, feedback, and resources to the liturgy director and music director as needed.
- Assist with and support the training of liturgical ministers.
-
-
-

Religious Education

- Support the director of religious education during implementation.
- Provide guidance, feedback, and resources to the director of religious education as needed.
- Assist with and support the training of catechists and parents.
-
-
-

School Board and PTA/PTO or Home-School Association

- Support the principal during implementation.
- Provide guidance, feedback, and resources to the principal as needed.
- Assist with and support the education of parents and school staff.
-
-
-

Youth Ministry

- Support the youth ministry director during implementation.
- Provide guidance, feedback, and resources to the youth ministry director as needed.
- Assist with and support the training of youth leaders and volunteer leaders.
-
-
-

WORKSHEET 2—PERSONAL EXPECTATIONS

Directions: Use the space provided to write down your reflections on each set of questions.

Why a new *Roman Missal* now?

✠ The Eucharist is the source and summit of Christian life.
✠ We have forty years of experience in celebrating the Liturgy in the vernacular.
✠ The revised text builds on that experience and offers a liturgical language marked by greater formality and dignity.
✠ The revised text draws more deeply on the rich Catholic theological Tradition, including Scripture and the works of the Fathers of the Church.

Reflection questions: What am I hoping to gain from my participation in the implementation of this new translation? What do I fear losing?

Why is catechesis about the *Roman Missal* important?

✠ The new translations use words filled with theological meaning. These words may be unfamiliar to many parishioners and require explanation.
✠ Parishioners may be uneasy about replacing texts long ago committed to memory. Catechesis can help to calm some anxiety.
✠ Catechesis can lead to a renewed understanding and appreciation of the Eucharistic Liturgy and its foundational role in the Christian life.

Reflection question: What do I need to learn to gain a deeper understanding of the *Roman Missal*?

What can the catechetical process for the *Roman Missal* bring to the parish or school?

✠ It will help us experience anew the importance of communion and of being one with the Church.
✠ It can lead parishioners to express their baptismal call in full, conscious, and active participation in the Liturgy.
✠ It provides an opportunity to examine the parish's liturgical practice and help all liturgical ministers develop a deeper understanding of the liturgical action.
✠ It can deepen our understanding and appreciation of the Liturgy, nurture liturgical practices that will lead to fuller liturgical participation, and help us celebrate the Liturgy with renewed purpose.

Reflection question: In what way will I commit to helping my parish or school implement the *Roman Missal*?

WORKSHEET 3—CREATING A STRATEGIC VISION STATEMENT

No.	Components	Parish or School Strategy Statement
1	**We advance our mission of**	Our parish or school mission: Prayer, worship, and catechetical dimensions:
2	**and seek to**	
3	**by serving**	
4	**in partnership with**	
5	**through**	
6	**and emphasizing our comparative advantage of**	
7	**We believe in**	

Copyright © La Piana Associates. Used and adapted with permission.

WORKSHEET 4—DEVELOPING GOALS AND OBJECTIVES

Goal 1		
To educate and train parish leaders to plan and implement a parish-wide program of liturgical formation and catechesis on the newly translated Mass.		
Priority	**Objectives**	**Measurement**
	❑ To identify the roles and responsibilities of key leaders for the parish implementation	
	❑ To set a schedule for implementing the parish Action Plan	
	❑ To communicate with the parish about the parish's Action Plan and about the changes themselves	
	❑ To make print, audio, video, and online resources available to leaders and parishioners	
	❑ To train the trainers at the parish level through print, in-person, and online resources	
	❑ To identify and develop camera-ready resources to promote general catechesis and liturgical formation on the changes in the Mass	
	❑	
	❑	
	❑	

Goal 2		
To help the faithful participate more fully, actively, and consciously in the Mass.		
Priority	**Objectives**	**Measurement**
	❏ To provide resources and tools to help the faithful practice the revised people's texts	
	❏ To train liturgical ministers so that they can lead the *Roman Missal* texts well	
	❏ To make connections, in preaching, between the newly translated texts and their scriptural roots as they appear naturally in the Lectionary cycle	
	❏ To plan opportunities for all parishioners to reflect on their roles as leaders of and participants in the Mass (e.g., as musicians, extraordinary ministers of Holy Communion, catechists, or parents)	
	❏ To encourage parish leaders (e.g., paid and volunteer catechists, youth ministers, and committee members) to plan and participate in sessions or experiences that focus on the Mass and their participation in it	
	❏	
	❏	
	❏	

Goal 3

Priority	Objectives	Measurement
	❑	
	❑	
	❑	

Goal 4

Priority	Objectives	Measurement
	❑	
	❑	
	❑	

Goal 5

Priority	Objectives	Measurement
	❑	
	❑	
	❑	

WORKSHEET 5—ACTION PLAN BY OBJECTIVE

Directions: Duplicate this form for each objective. Use one form per objective. Once the activities are listed, prioritize them.

Action Plan Worksheet			
Implementation of the *Roman Missal*			
Goal:			
Objective:			
Measurement:			
Activities	**Timeline**	**Resources Needed**	**Responsible Person/Team**

WORKSHEET 6—TWELVE-MONTH PLANNING CALENDAR

	For Leadership and Ministries	For Parishioners
First Quarter: Months 12 to 10		
Second Quarter: Months 9 to 7		
Third Quarter: Months 6 to 4		
Final Quarter: Months 3 to 1		

HANDOUT 1—KEY DOCUMENTS

Purpose and Nature of the Liturgy (Mass)

Second Vatican Council. *Constitution on the Sacred Liturgy* (*Sacrosanctum Concilium*). Available in several editions, including one on the Vatican Web site (*www.vatican.va*).

Pope John Paul II. *On the Eucharist* (*Ecclesia de Eucharistia*). Washington, DC: USCCB, 2003. Also available on the Vatican Web site (*www.vatican.va*).

Pope Benedict XVI. *The Sacrament of Charity* (*Sacramentum Caritatis*). Washington, DC: USCCB, 2007. Also available on the Vatican Web site (*www.vatican.va*).

Parts of the Mass

General Instruction of the Roman Missal. Washington, DC: USCCB, 2003. Also available at the *Roman Missal* Web site: *www.usccb.org/romanmissal.*

Introduction to the Lectionary. Available in the front of your parish's or school's lectionary.

USCCB Committee on Divine Worship. *Introduction to the Order of Mass.* Pastoral Liturgy Series 1. Washington, DC: USCCB, 2003.

USCCB. *Built of Living Stones: Art, Architecture, and Worship.* Washington, DC: USCCB, 2005.

USCCB. *Sing to the Lord: Music in Divine Worship.* Pastoral Liturgy Series 4. Washington, DC: USCCB, 2007.

Purpose and Reason for the Revision

✠ *Roman Missal* Web site (*www.usccb.org/romanmissal*).

✠ *With One Voice: Translation and Implementation of the Third Edition of the Roman Missal.* Washington, DC: Federation of Diocesan Liturgical Commissions, 2010.

✠ *Become One Body, One Spirit in Christ.* A multimedia resource from the Leeds Group (information is available at *www.usccbpublishing.org*).

HANDOUT 2—OPENING AND CLOSING PRAYERS

Opening Prayer

Lord Jesus Christ,
you call us to worship the Father
in Spirit and in truth.
Send your Spirit upon us
as we reflect upon the Eucharistic Liturgy,
the celebration of your Paschal Mystery.
May the liturgy make us one Body in you
and lead us to your table in heaven.
Amen.

Closing Prayer

Lord Jesus Christ,
you offered yourself on the Cross to save us from our sins,
and you gave us the Eucharist as a memorial of your sacrifice.
May we always celebrate this memorial
with all our whole heart and mind and soul
that we may be worthy of celebrating with you in heaven,
where you reign with the Father and the Holy Spirit,
now and for ever.
Amen.

HANDOUT 3—COMPONENTS OF A STRATEGIC VISION STATEMENT

We advance our mission of [_____]

and seek to [_____]

by serving [_____]

in partnership with [_____]

through [_____]

and emphasizing our comparative advantage of [_____].

We believe in [_____].

APPENDICES

This section of the *Parish Guide to Implementing the Roman Missal, Third Edition,* contains resources that parishes and schools can use during the proximate catechetical period. These include resources developed by the USCCB, FDLC, the Leeds Group, and other Catholic publishing houses.

APPENDIX A

GLOSSARY OF TERMS

PART I: GENERAL

Assembly, liturgical: All of the faithful—priest, assisting ministers, and congregation—gathered for the celebration of the Mass or one of the other liturgical-sacramental rites of the Church. The liturgical assembly does not constitute itself but is called into being by God.

Catechesis: The education of children, young people, and adults in the faith of the Church through the teaching of Christian doctrine in an organic and systematic way to make them disciples of Jesus Christ. (See also **Liturgical catechesis.**)

Celebrant: The one, normally a bishop or priest or, in certain circumstances, a deacon, who officiates and presides over the celebration of the Liturgy.

Congregation for Divine Worship and the Discipline of the Sacraments (CDWDS): The department of the Holy See responsible for regulating and promoting the Church's sacred Liturgy and sacraments; the CDWDS also reviews, revises, and approves liturgical texts and translations.

Dynamic equivalency: A translation principle that aims to translate basic thoughts rather than words. The original words and form are important only as a vehicle for the meaning; therefore, it is the meaning alone that is truly important in the translation. This

method was used during the preparation of the first and second editions of the *Roman Missal*, but it was gradually refined in the ensuing years and ultimately was replaced in 2001 in favor of the principle of formal equivalency.

***Editio typica* (typical edition):** The official Latin text of a liturgical book or church document (e.g., the *Catechism of the Catholic Church* or a papal encyclical) from which vernacular translations are written. *Editio typica tertia* is Latin for "third typical edition," the version of the *Roman Missal* being implemented in late 2011.

Eucharistic Prayer: This prayer is the summit of the celebration of the Mass. It is a prayer of thanksgiving and sanctification. The word "Eucharist" comes from the Greek and is literally translated as "thanksgiving." The entire congregation of the faithful joins itself to Christ in offering sacrifice to God, and in turn Christ is offered to the Church in his Body and Blood.

Formal equivalency: A translation principle approved by the CDWDS in its 2001 document *Liturgiam Authenticam* for use in the third edition of the *Roman Missal* and all future liturgical books. This method aims to translate texts "integrally and in the most exact manner, without omissions or additions in terms of their content, and without paraphrases or glosses" (*Liturgiam Authenticam*, no. 201). The original Latin text is thereby rendered into English more literally.

General Instruction of the Roman Missal (GIRM): The introductory material in the *Roman Missal*, containing the general outline and ordering of the celebration of the Mass, including detailed instructions about what the priest, the deacon, the other ministers, and the congregation do during the various parts of the Mass.

International Commission on English in the Liturgy (ICEL): Committee chartered to prepare English translations of liturgical texts on behalf of the conferences of bishops of English-speaking countries. Currently, eleven conferences of bishops are full members of the commission: the United States, Australia, Canada, England and Wales, India, Ireland, New Zealand, Pakistan, the Philippines, Scotland, and South Africa.

Liturgiam Authenticam: Document issued in 2001 by the CDWDS that discusses the use of vernacular languages in the publication of the books of the Roman Liturgy, providing the guiding principles for translation.

Liturgical catechesis: "Liturgical catechesis aims to initiate people into the mystery of Christ (It is 'mystagogy.') by proceeding from the visible to the invisible, from the sign to the thing signified, from the 'sacraments' to the 'mysteries'" (CCC, no. 1075).

Mandatory use date: The date on which a liturgical text must be used in worship. After this date, previous texts may not be licitly used.

Mystagogy: From the Greek meaning "deepening in" or "educating in the mysteries," "a liturgical catechesis [which] aims to initiate people into the mystery of Christ" (CCC, no. 1075). In a more specific sense, the catechetical period following immediately after the reception of Baptism by adults.

Patristics: The writings of the holy Fathers of the Church of the first centuries. These Fathers are privileged witnesses of the apostolic tradition.

Promulgation: The formal publication of an ecclesial text.

Ratio Translationis: A document issued by the CDWDS in which the principles of translation found in *Liturgiam Authenticam* are applied in closer detail to a given language. This document may be composed of various elements that the situation may require, such as a list of vernacular words to be equated with their Latin counterparts, principles applicable specifically to a given language, and so forth.

Recognitio: An authoritative approval of texts that grants permission for their use. For liturgical texts, *recognitio* is usually issued by the Vatican Congregation for Divine Worship and the Discipline of the Sacraments.

Roman Missal/Missale Romanum: The ritual text for the celebration of the Mass, which contains the words and actions completed by the assembly and the celebrant during Mass. *Missale Romanum* is the name of the Latin text of the *Roman Missal*.

Rubrics: The directions given for how to celebrate Mass and other liturgical ceremonies, including preparations, postures, gestures, and movement. The word "rubric" comes from the Latin word for "red" because these instructions are typically printed in red type to distinguish them from texts to be spoken.

Sacramentary: The name given to the English translation of the *Roman Missal* in its current edition published in 1974 and revised in 1985. In the first millennium of Christianity, the book that contained the prayers for Mass as well as the other sacraments was often called a sacramentary. The new text containing the prayers of the Mass is more accurately called the *Roman Missal*.

Sacrosanctum Concilium (*Constitution on the Sacred Liturgy*): The first document issued by the Fathers of the Second Vatican Council in December 1963. This constitution established the basic goals and directives governing the renewal of the Liturgy in the Latin Church.

USCCB Committee on Divine Worship: The committee established by the United States Catholic Conference of Bishops to assist the bishops of the Latin Church, both collectively and individually, in fulfilling their roles as priests and leaders of the worshiping community, especially with the translation of liturgical text and the development of guidelines for the celebration of the Mass and the sacraments. The committee is assisted by the staff of the Secretariat of Divine Worship, which assists in the day-to-day work of the committee and in the carrying out of the goals and objectives of the committee.

Vernacular: The language(s) commonly spoken by the people of a region.

Vox Clara: Taking its name from the Latin words meaning "clear voice," this committee of bishops from around the English-speaking world was established by the CDWDS in 2001 to advise the Congregation in its responsibilities related to the translation of liturgical texts in the English language and to strengthen effective cooperation with the conferences of bishops.

PART II: PARTS OF THE MASS

Entries in this section are given in the order in which they occur in the Mass.

Introductory Rites: "The rites that precede the Liturgy of the Word, namely, the Entrance, the Greeting, the Penitential Act, the *Kyrie*, the *Glória in excélsis (Glory to God in the highest)* and Collect, have the character of a beginning, an introduction, and a preparation. Their purpose is to ensure that the faithful who come together as one, establish communion and dispose themselves properly to listen to the word of God and to celebrate the Eucharist worthily" (*General Instruction of the Roman Missal* [GIRM], no. 46).

Collect: "The [opening] prayer . . . through which the character of the celebration finds expression" (GIRM, no. 54). This prayer literally "collects" the prayers of all who are gathered into one prayer led by the priest celebrant.

Liturgy of the Word: "The main part of the Liturgy of the Word is made up of the readings from Sacred Scripture together with the chants occurring between them. As for the Homily, the Profession of Faith and the Universal Prayer, they develop and conclude it" (GIRM, no. 55).

Creed: A brief, normative summary statement or profession of Christian faith. The Nicene Creed, which is recited or chanted at Mass, comes from the Councils of Nicea (AD 325) and Constantinople (AD 381).

Canon of the Mass: The central part of the Mass, also known as the Eucharistic Prayer or anaphora, which is the prayer of thanksgiving and consecration. It begins with the Preface Dialogue (i.e., "The Lord be with you . . . . Lift up your hearts . . . . Let us give thanks to the Lord our God") and concludes with a final Doxology ("Through him, and with him, and in him") and Amen.

Epiclesis: The prayer petitioning the Father to send the Holy Spirit to sanctify offerings of bread and wine so that they may become the Body and Blood of Christ.

Consecration: The consecration is that part of the Eucharistic Prayer during which the priest prays the Lord's words of institution of the Eucharist at the Last Supper. Through this prayer the bread and wine become the risen Body and Blood of Jesus.

Anamnesis: From the Greek meaning "remembrance." We remember Jesus' historical saving deeds in the liturgical action of the Church, which inspires thanksgiving and praise. Every Eucharistic Prayer contains an anamnesis or memorial in which the Church calls to mind the Passion, Resurrection, and glorious return of Christ Jesus.

Doxology: A Christian prayer that gives praise and glory to God, often in a special way to the three divine Persons of the Trinity. Liturgical prayers, including the Eucharistic Prayer, traditionally conclude with the Doxology "to the Father, through the Son, in the Holy Spirit."

Communion Rite: The preparatory rites, consisting of the Lord's Prayer, the Rite of Peace, and the Fraction, lead the faithful to Holy Communion (see GIRM, no. 80). The Prayer After Communion expresses the Church's gratitude for the mysteries celebrated and received.

Rite of Peace: The rite "by which the Church entreats peace and unity for herself and for the whole human family, and the faithful express to each other their ecclesial communion and mutual charity before communicating in the Sacrament" (GIRM, no. 82).

Fraction: "The priest breaks the Eucharistic Bread. . . . The gesture of breaking bread done by Christ at the Last Supper . . . in apostolic times gave the entire Eucharistic Action its name" (GIRM, no. 83).

Communion: Holy Communion, the reception of the Body and Blood of Christ in the Eucharist.

Concluding Rites: "To the Concluding Rites belong the following: brief announcements … ; the priest's greeting and blessing … ; the dismissal of the people by the deacon or the priest, so that each may go back to doing good works, praising and blessing God; the kissing of the altar by the priest and the deacon, followed by a profound bow to the altar by the priest, the deacon, and the other ministers" (GIRM, no. 90).

PART III: PARTS OF THE *ROMAN MISSAL*

The *Roman Missal* has seven major sections, plus introductory material (various decrees and papal letters, the *General Instruction of the Roman Missal*, and the liturgical calendar) and appendices (additional chants, various blessings, sample General Intercessions, and optional prayers by the priest before and after Mass). This list defines those major sections in order of appearance.

Order of Mass (*Ordo Missae*): The overall structure of the Mass and the fixed parts of the Mass (those that are the same at every Mass), including the responses and acclamations of the people, the introductory rites, the Eucharistic Prayer (including the collection of Prefaces), the prayers leading up to Holy Communion, and the concluding rites, including Solemn Blessings and Prayers over the People.

Proper of Seasons: Mass formularies (containing the opening Collect prayer, the Prayer over the Offerings, the Prayer After Communion, and sometimes a Solemn Blessing) for the Sundays and weekdays of the seasons of Advent, Christmas, Lent, and Easter; the Sundays of Ordinary Time; and major feast days.

Proper of Saints (and the Commons): Prayers for the feast days of the various saints commemorated throughout the year, and a collection of prayers for use to honor a saint for whom no proper prayers are included.

Ritual Masses: Prayers for Masses that are celebrated with particular rites, such as the dedication of a church, the Sacrament of Marriage, the Sacrament of Holy Orders, religious profession, and Christian initiation (Sacraments of Baptism and Confirmation).

Masses and Prayers for Various Needs and Intentions: Prayers for Masses celebrated for particular religious or civil needs, such as for the pope, for vocations, for the promotion of harmony, for peace and justice, for elected officials, for the aversion of storms, and so forth.

Votive Masses: Prayers for Masses for particular devotions such as Masses in honor of the Holy Spirit, the Blessed Virgin Mary, or the Apostles.

Masses of the Dead: Prayers for funeral Masses or other commemorations of those who have died, particularly on the anniversary of death.

APPENDIX B

HOMILY HELPS

(Key Reflection Points from Catechetical Sunday 2011 through Christmas 2011)

The following brief notes for each Sunday in the months before and immediately after the implementation of the *Roman Missal, Third Edition*, are derived from the Lectionary readings for the day. These notes will help homilists, catechists who are responsible for breaking open the Word for catechumens, and others who lead reflection groups on the Sunday readings to invite the faithful to a renewed participation in the Liturgy and to a deeper relationship with the Lord in the Eucharist.

September 18, 2011: Twenty-Fifth Sunday in Ordinary Time

✠ The Lord's ways are not our ways, nor are his thoughts our thoughts. In a few months, we will begin using a revised missal. The language may seem awkward and unfamiliar, but it will assist us in developing a liturgical language that reflects the dignity of the mysteries we celebrate.

✠ St. Paul calls on us to magnify Christ by our living and our dying. In Liturgy—the work of the people—we magnify Christ by uniting the joys and sorrows of our daily living to his perfect sacrifice of praise and thanksgiving to the Father.

September 25, 2011: Twenty-Sixth Sunday in Ordinary Time

✠ In the Sacred Liturgy, we join with the faithful in all times and places to "confess that Jesus Christ is Lord, to the glory of God the Father" (Phil 2:11).

✠ In the Eucharistic Liturgy, we gather as the Body of Christ to be "united in heart, thinking one thing" (Phil 2:2).

✠ "Full, conscious, and active participation" (SC, no. 14) in the Liturgy forms us in the way of righteousness, so that our words and actions may be one.

October 2, 2011: Twenty-Seventh Sunday in Ordinary Time

✠ We gather in the Liturgy in order to, "by prayer and petition, with thanksgiving, make [our] requests known to God" (Phil 4:6). We offer our lives in loving service to God and to his people, and we ask God in humble trust for all we need.

✠ Strengthened by our common celebration and by receiving the Body and Blood of Christ, our faith must bear fruit.

October 9, 2011: Twenty-Eighth Sunday in Ordinary Time

✠ The Eucharistic Liturgy we celebrate each Sunday is a foretaste of the heavenly banquet, the wedding feast of the Lamb, described in today's readings.

✠ At the eucharistic table, all are equal. There must be no division of wealth, race, or nation. All who believe must join in giving praise and worship to the Father through the Son and in the Spirit.

✠ As the guest must come with his wedding garment, we must come with our hearts and minds prepared to participate fully in the Liturgy.

October 16, 2011: Twenty-Ninth Sunday in Ordinary Time

✠ In his first Letter to the Thessalonians, Paul expresses "thanks to God always for all of you, remembering you in our prayers" (1 Thes 1:2). In the Eucharistic Liturgy, we join with the clergy and faithful throughout the world to pray for the needs of the Church and the world.

✠ By participating fully in the Liturgy, we offer to God what belongs to God by uniting our prayers, our actions, and our very selves to Christ's perfect oblation of praise and thanksgiving.

October 23, 2011: Thirtieth Sunday in Ordinary Time

✠ The greatest commandment describes the "full, conscious, and active" participation in the Liturgy to which we are all called (SC, no. 14). We must take part in the Liturgy with all our heart, with all our soul, and with all our mind.

✠ Through our participation in the Liturgy and our reception of the Eucharist, we must be conformed ever more closely to Christ. As we receive Christ truly present in the Eucharist, we must strive to imitate him ever more closely.

October 30, 2011: Thirty-First Sunday in Ordinary Time

✠ Through the celebration of the Eucharistic Liturgy, the Church throughout the world gives "thanks to God unceasingly." The fruits of the Liturgy should likewise be "at work in [all] who believe" (1 Thes 2:13).

✠ In the Gospel, Jesus warns about those who burden others without offering to assist. In the second reading, Paul highlights the care and gentleness with which he approached those to whom he was called. As the implementation of the revised Liturgy draws near, it is important to recognize the unease that some people may feel about the changes and gently help these people to accept the changes with an open heart and mind.

November 6, 2011: Thirty-Second Sunday in Ordinary Time

✠ Today's Gospel is a parable about being prepared. As the wise virgins were prepared to enter the wedding feast with the bridegroom, so too must we prepare to celebrate the wedding feast of the Lamb worthily and well.

✠ The reading from the Book of Wisdom invites the faithful to seek wisdom in all things. The revised texts of the Liturgy may seem strange to our ears at first, but we must prudently take the time to seek out the deeper meanings they convey.

November 13, 2011: Thirty-Third Sunday in Ordinary Time

✠ God calls us to be prudent with the gifts given to us, guarding them carefully, yet using them well. The Liturgy is the great treasure of the Church. The Church takes great care to ensure that the Liturgy, in every age, expresses the truths of our faith, strengthens the faithful in their Christian living, and, through Christ and in the Spirit, offers a worthy sacrifice to the Father.

✠ Although the form of the Liturgy may differ in various times and places, it remains a witness to an unchanged faith and an unbroken tradition (see the *General Instruction of the Roman Missal*, Preamble).

November 20, 2011: Solemnity of Christ the King

✠ Today's gospel reading reminds us once again of the essential relationship between the Eucharistic Liturgy and Christian living. Those who worship and receive the Body of Christ in the Eucharist are called to serve him in the lowliest and most vulnerable members of society.

✠ In times of struggle, pain, and confusion, we turn our hearts and minds to the Lord, who, in his Church, will shepherd us along the path that leads to life.

✠ In our liturgy and our living, we have but one goal: "that God may be all in all" (1 Cor 15:28).

Sundays of Advent

The First Sunday of Advent will mark the first use of the *Roman Missal*. In these first few weeks, it will be important to recognize people's unease with the revised texts while still maintaining the full celebration of the Eucharistic Liturgy and the Advent season. These homily tips may help:

✠ Although each Advent marks the beginning of a new liturgical year, this Advent marks the beginning of a renewed moment in the Church's liturgical life. In Advent, we prepare for the coming of Christ at Christmas and at the end of time. So should we intensify our participation in the Eucharistic Liturgy to prepare for the coming of Christ into our hearts in the Holy Eucharist.

✠ Use the Collect or Preface as a principal text for the homily. In the first two weeks of Advent, these texts focus on the twofold coming of Christ—as a child at Christmas and in glory at the end of time. In the last two weeks, these texts will focus more specifically on preparing to celebrate the Incarnation of Jesus, emphasizing its necessary relationship to the Paschal Mystery we celebrate in the Eucharistic Liturgy.

APPENDIX C

NOVENA FOR A FULLER PARTICIPATION IN THE SACRAMENT OF THE EUCHARIST

Parishes, schools, groups, or individuals may use the following novena. It should include time for sacred silence and may be supplemented with appropriate songs. (The prayers in this novena are excerpted from the *Roman Missal, Third Edition*.)

You may use this novena in a variety of ways. Parishes may use it on the same day (e.g., the First Friday) for each of the nine months preceding the first use of the *Roman Missal*; on the same weekday for nine weeks preceding the first use; or for nine consecutive days, multiple times throughout the implementation. The nine days might be celebrated instead as the various hours of eucharistic adoration. A parish group might use the novena as the opening prayer for its meetings. The novena might be used before or after daily Mass in a parish. Families and individuals might use the novena as part of their prayer at table, as a prayer before bed, or at the conclusion of the family Rosary.

Day One: That priests will celebrate the Eucharist worthily.

Leader: **In the name of the Father, and of the Son, and of the Holy Spirit.**

All: Amen.

Scripture Reading Genesis 14:18-20 (LFM 976.1)

Melchizedek brought out bread and wine.

A reading from the Book of Genesis

Melchizedek, king of Salem, brought out bread and wine,
   and being a priest of God Most High,
   he blessed Abram with these words:
"Blessed be Abram by God Most High,
   the creator of heaven and earth;
And blessed be God Most High,
   who delivered your foes into your hand."
Then Abram gave him a tenth of everything.

The word of the Lord.

Reflection

"The Lord entrusts to you [priests] the mystery of this Sacrament [Eucharist]. In his Name you can say: 'This is my Body.... . This is my Blood.' Allow yourselves to be drawn ever anew by the Holy Eucharist, by communion of life with Christ. Consider the center of each day the possibility to celebrate the Eucharist worthily. Lead people ever anew to this mystery. Help them, starting from this, to bring the peace of Christ into the world" (Pope Benedict XVI, Homily at Mass and priestly ordinations on Pentecost, May 15, 2005).

(A time of sacred silence should be observed.)

Leader:

**O God, who made your Only-Begotten Son eternal High Priest,
grant that those he has chosen
as ministers and stewards of your mysteries
may be found faithful in carrying out
the ministry they have received.
Through our Lord Jesus Christ, your Son,
who lives and reigns with you and the Holy Spirit,
one God, forever and ever.**

Novena Prayer

Prayer of Self-Offering

Receive, Lord, my entire freedom.
Accept the whole of my memory,
my intellect and my will.
Whatever I have or possess,
it was you who gave it to me;
I restore it to you in full,
and I surrender it completely
to the guidance of your will.
Give me only love of you
together with your grace,
and I am rich enough,
and ask for nothing more.
Amen.

Day Two: That all will celebrate the Eucharist with wholehearted trust in God.

Leader: **In the name of the Father, and of the Son, and of the Holy Spirit.**

All: Amen.

Scripture Reading   Genesis 22:1-18 (LFM 41)

The sacrifice of Abraham our father in faith.

A reading from the Book of Genesis

God put Abraham to the test.
He called to him, "Abraham!"
"Here I am," he replied.
Then God said:
    "Take your son Isaac, your only one, whom you love,
    and go to the land of Moriah.
There you shall offer him up as a holocaust
    on a height that I will point out to you."
Early the next morning Abraham saddled his donkey,
    took with him his son Isaac and two of his
        servants as well,
    and with the wood that he had cut for the holocaust,
    set out for the place of which God had told him.

On the third day Abraham got sight of the place
    from afar.
Then he said to his servants:
    "Both of you stay here with the donkey,
    while the boy and I go on over yonder.
We will worship and then come back to you."
Thereupon Abraham took the wood for the holocaust
    and laid it on his son Isaac's shoulders,
    while he himself carried the fire and the knife.
As the two walked on together, Isaac spoke to his
    father Abraham:
    "Father!" Isaac said.
"Yes, son," he replied.
Isaac continued, "Here are the fire and the wood,
    but where is the sheep for the holocaust?"
"Son," Abraham answered,

"God himself will provide the sheep for the holocaust."
Then the two continued going forward.

When they came to the place of which God had told him,
    Abraham built an altar there and arranged the wood on it.
Next he tied up his son Isaac,
    and put him on top of the wood on the altar.
Then he reached out and took the knife to slaughter his son.
But the Lord's messenger called to him from heaven, "Abraham, Abraham!"
"Here I am!" he answered.
"Do not lay your hand on the boy," said the messenger.
"Do not do the least thing to him.
I know now how devoted you are to God,
    since you did not withhold from me your own beloved son."
As Abraham looked about,
    he spied a ram caught by its horns in the thicket.
So he went and took the ram
    and offered it up as a holocaust in place of his son.
Abraham named the site Yahweh-yireh;
    hence people now say, "On the mountain the Lord will see."
Again the Lord's messenger called to Abraham from heaven and said:
    "I swear by myself, declares the Lord,
    that because you acted as you did
    in not withholding from me your beloved son,
    I will bless you abundantly
    and make your descendants as countless
    as the stars of the sky and the sands of the seashore;
    your descendants shall take possession
    of the gates of their enemies,
    and in your descendants all the nations of the earth shall find blessing—
    all this because you obeyed my command."

The word of the Lord.

Reflection

"Christ gives us his Body in the Eucharist, he gives himself in his Body and thus makes us his Body, he unites us with his Risen Body. If man eats ordinary bread, in the digestive process this bread becomes part of his body, transformed into a substance of human life. But in holy Communion the inverse process is brought about. Christ, the Lord, assimilates us into himself, introducing us into his glorious Body, and thus we all become his Body" (Pope Benedict XVI, General Audience, December 10, 2008).

(A time of sacred silence should be observed.)

Leader:

**Grant, O Lord, that your servants,
gathered in your love
and partaking of the one Bread,
may be of one heart in prompting each other
in the pursuit of charity and good works,
so that through a holy way of life
they may always and everywhere
be true witnesses to Christ.
Who lives and reigns for ever and ever.**

Novena Prayer
Prayer of Self-Offering

Receive, Lord, my entire freedom.
Accept the whole of my memory,
my intellect and my will.
Whatever I have or possess,
it was you who gave it to me;
I restore it to you in full,
and I surrender it completely
to the guidance of your will.
Give me only love of you
together with your grace,
and I am rich enough,
and ask for nothing more.
Amen.

Day Three: That parents will help lead their children to more conscious and active participation in the Eucharist.

Leader: **In the name of the Father, and of the Son, and of the Holy Spirit.**

All: Amen.

Scripture Reading   Exodus 12:1-8, 11-14 (LFM 39)

The law regarding the Passover meal.

A reading from the Book of Exodus

The LORD said to Moses and Aaron in the land of Egypt,
  "This month shall stand at the head of your calendar;
    you shall reckon it the first month of the year.
Tell the whole community of Israel:
    On the tenth of this month every one of your families
    must procure for itself a lamb, one apiece for each household.
If a family is too small for a whole lamb,
    it shall join the nearest household in procuring one
    and shall share in the lamb
    in proportion to the number of persons who partake of it.
The lamb must be a year-old male and without blemish.
You may take it from either the sheep or the goats.
You shall keep it until the fourteenth day of this month,
    and then, with the whole assembly of Israel present,
    it shall be slaughtered during the evening twilight.
They shall take some of its blood
    and apply it to the two doorposts and the lintel
    of every house in which they partake of the lamb.
That same night they shall eat its roasted flesh
    with unleavened bread and bitter herbs.

"This is how you are to eat it:
    with your loins girt, sandals on your feet and your staff in hand,
    you shall eat like those who are in flight.
It is the Passover of the LORD.
For on this same night I will go through Egypt,
    striking down every firstborn of the land, both man and beast,
    and executing judgment on all the gods of Egypt—I, the LORD!
But the blood will mark the houses where you are.
Seeing the blood, I will pass over you;
    thus, when I strike the land of Egypt,
    no destructive blow will come upon you.

"This day shall be a memorial feast for you,
    which all your generations shall celebrate
    with pilgrimage to the Lord, as a perpetual institution."

The word of the Lord.

Reflection

"Dear parents! I ask you to help your children to grow in faith, I ask you to accompany them on their journey towards First Communion, a journey which continues beyond that day, and to keep accompanying them as they make their way to Jesus and with Jesus. Please, go with your children to Church and take part in the Sunday eucharistic celebration! You will see that this is not time lost; rather, it is the very thing that can keep your family truly united and centered. Sunday becomes more beautiful, the whole week becomes more beautiful, when you go to Sunday Mass together" (Pope Benedict XVI, Homily at Mass in Munich, September 10, 2006).

(A time of sacred silence should be observed.)

Leader:

**O God, in whose eternal design
family life has its firm foundation,
look with compassion on the prayers of your servants
and grant that, following the example
of the Holy Family of your Only-Begotten Son
in practicing the virtues of family life
and in the bonds of charity,
we may, in the joy of your house,
delight one day in eternal rewards.**

Through our Lord Jesus Christ, your Son,
who lives and reigns with you and the Holy Spirit,
one God, forever and ever.

Novena Prayer

Prayer of Self-Offering

Receive, Lord, my entire freedom.
Accept the whole of my memory,
my intellect and my will.
Whatever I have or possess,
it was you who gave it to me;
I restore it to you in full,
and I surrender it completely
to the guidance of your will.
Give me only love of you
together with your grace,
and I am rich enough,
and ask for nothing more.
Amen.

Day Four: That our participation in the Eucharistic Liturgy will lead us to greater care for all members of the Body of Christ.

Leader: **In the name of the Father, and of the Son, and of the Holy Spirit.**

All: Amen.

Scripture Reading   Luke 9:11b-17 (LFM 981.3)

They all ate and were satisfied.

✠ A reading from the holy Gospel according to Luke

Jesus spoke to the crowds about the Kingdom of God,
    and he healed those who needed to be cured.
As the day was drawing to a close,
    the Twelve approached him and said,
    "Dismiss the crowd
    so that they can go to the surrounding villages
        and farms
    and find lodging and provisions;
    for we are in a deserted place here."

He said to them, "Give them some food yourselves."
They replied, "Five loaves and two fish are all we have,
    unless we ourselves go and buy food for all these
        people."
Now the men there numbered about five thousand.
Then he said to his disciples,
    "Have them sit down in groups of about fifty."
They did so and made them all sit down.
Then taking the five loaves and the two fish,
    and looking up to heaven,
        he said the blessing over them, broke them,
        and gave them to the disciples to set before the
            crowd.
They all ate and were satisfied.
And when the leftover fragments were picked up,
    they filled twelve wicker baskets.

The Gospel of the Lord.

Reflection

"'The cup of blessing which we bless, is it not a participation in the Blood of Christ? The bread which we break, is it not a participation in the Body of Christ? Because there is one bread, we who are many are one body, for we all partake of the one bread' (1 Cor 10:16-17). In these words the personal and social character of the Sacrament of the Eucharist likewise appears. Christ personally unites himself with each one of us, but Christ himself is also united with the man and the woman who are next to me. And the bread is for me but it is also for the other. Thus Christ unites all of us with himself and all of us with one another. In communion we receive Christ. But Christ is likewise united with my neighbor: Christ and my neighbor are inseparable in the Eucharist. And thus we are all one bread and one body. A Eucharist without solidarity with others is a Eucharist abused. And here we come to the root and, at the same time, the kernel of the doctrine on the Church as the Body of Christ, of the Risen Christ" (Pope Benedict XVI, General Audience, December 10, 2008).

(A time of sacred silence should be observed.)

Leader:

**As we draw upon the fullness of your grace,
we pray, O Lord,
that your faithful,
who by your will are engaged in the things of
  this world,
may be strengthened by the power of the
  Eucharistic Banquet,
to be tireless witnesses to the truth of the Gospel
and may ever make your Church present and active
amid the affairs of this age.
Through our Lord Jesus Christ, your Son,
who lives and reigns with you and the Holy Spirit,
one God, forever and ever.**

Novena Prayer

Prayer of Self-Offering

Receive, Lord, my entire freedom.
Accept the whole of my memory,
my intellect and my will.
Whatever I have or possess,
it was you who gave it to me;
I restore it to you in full,
and I surrender it completely
to the guidance of your will.
Give me only love of you
together with your grace,
and I am rich enough,
and ask for nothing more.
Amen.

Day Five: That those in consecrated life will keep the Eucharist at the center of their lives.

Leader: **In the name of the Father, and of the Son, and of the Holy Spirit.**

All: Amen.

Scripture Reading   John 6:51-58 (LFM 981.9)

My Flesh is true food and my Blood is true drink.

✠ A reading from the holy Gospel according to John

Jesus said to the Jews who were present:
"I am the living bread that came down from heaven;
  whoever eats this bread will live forever;
  and the bread that I will give
  is my Flesh for the life of the world."

The Jews quarreled among themselves, saying,
  "How can this man give us his Flesh to eat?"
Jesus said to them,
  "Amen, amen, I say to you,
  unless you eat the Flesh of the Son of Man and
    drink his Blood,
  you do not have life within you.
Whoever eats my Flesh and drinks my Blood
  has eternal life,
  and I will raise him on the last day.
For my Flesh is true food,
  and my Blood is true drink.
Whoever eats my Flesh and drinks my Blood
  remains in me and I in him
Just as the living Father sent me
  and I have life because of the Father,
  so also the one who feeds on me
  will have life because of me.
This is the bread that came down from heaven.
Unlike your ancestors who ate and still died,
  whoever eats this bread will live forever."

The Gospel of the Lord.

Reflection

"The Eucharist—the center of our Christian being—is founded on Jesus' sacrifice for us; it is born from the suffering of love which culminated in the Cross. We live by this love that gives itself. It gives us the courage and strength to suffer with Christ and for him in this world, knowing that in this very way our life becomes great and mature and true" (Pope Benedict XVI, Homily at Mass for the Opening of the Year of Saint Paul, June 28, 2008).

(A time of sacred silence should be observed.)

Leader:

O God, who inspire and bring to fulfillment
    every good intention,
direct your servants into the way of eternal salvation,
and as they have left all things
to devote themselves entirely to you,
grant that,
following Christ and renouncing the things of
    this world,
they may faithfully serve you and their neighbor
in a spirit of poverty and in humility of heart.
Through our Lord Jesus Christ, your Son,
who lives and reigns with you and the Holy Spirit,
one God, forever and ever.

Novena Prayer

Prayer of Self-Offering

Receive, Lord, my entire freedom.
Accept the whole of my memory,
my intellect and my will.
Whatever I have or possess,
it was you who gave it to me;
I restore it to you in full,
and I surrender it completely
to the guidance of your will.
Give me only love of you
together with your grace,
and I am rich enough,
and ask for nothing more.
Amen.

Day Six: That the Eucharistic Liturgy will be a source of strength and hope for all the faithful.

Leader: **In the name of the Father, and of the Son,
    and of the Holy Spirit.**

All: Amen.

Scripture Reading Mark 14:12-16, 22-26 (LFM 981.1)

This is my Body. This is my Blood.

✠ A reading from the holy Gospel according to Mark

On the first day of the Feast of Unleavened Bread,
    when they sacrificed the Passover Lamb,
    the disciples of Jesus said to him,
    "Where do you want us to go
    and prepare for you to eat the Passover?"
He sent two of his disciples and said to them,
    "Go into the city and a man will meet you,
    carrying a jar of water.
Follow him.
Wherever he enters, say to the master of the house,
    'The Teacher says, "Where is my guest room
    where I may eat the Passover with my disciples?"'
Then he will show you a large upper room furnished
    and ready.
Make the preparations for us there."
The disciples then went off, entered the city,
    and found it just as he had told them;
    and they prepared the Passover.

While they were eating,
    he took bread, said the blessing,
    broke it, gave it to them, and said,
    "Take it; this is my Body."
Then he took a cup, gave thanks, and gave it to them,
    and they all drank from it.
He said to them,
    "This is my Blood of the covenant,
    which will be shed for many.
Amen, I say to you,
    I shall not drink again the fruit of the vine
    until the day when I drink it new in the Kingdom
    of God."
Then, after singing a hymn,
    they went out to the Mount of Olives.

The Gospel of the Lord.

Reflection

"The Eucharist is our most beautiful treasure. It is
the Sacrament *par excellence*; it ushers us into eternal
life in advance; it contains the entire mystery of our
salvation; it is the source and summit of the action
and life of the Church as the Second Vatican Council
recalled (cf. *Sacrosanctum Concilium*, no. 8). It is

therefore particularly important that pastors and faithful be constantly committed to deepening their knowledge of this great Sacrament. In this way each one will be able to affirm his faith and carry out his mission in the Church and in the world ever better, remembering that the Eucharist bears fruit in one's personal life, in the life of the Church and the world" (Pope Benedict XVI, Homily delivered by satellite for the closing of the forty-ninth International Eucharistic Congress in Quebec, June 22, 2008).

(A time of sacred silence should be observed.)

Leader:

**O God, in the covenant of your Christ
you never cease to gather to yourself from all
nations
a people growing together in unity through the
Spirit;
grant, we pray, that your Church,
faithful to the mission entrusted to her,
may continually go forward with the human family
and always be the leaven and the soul of human
society,
to renew it in Christ and transform it into the
family of God.
Through our Lord Jesus Christ, your Son,
who lives and reigns with you and the Holy Spirit,
one God, forever and ever.**

Novena Prayer

Prayer of Self-Offering

Receive, Lord, my entire freedom.
Accept the whole of my memory,
my intellect and my will.
Whatever I have or possess,
it was you who gave it to me;
I restore it to you in full,
and I surrender it completely
to the guidance of your will.
Give me only love of you
together with your grace,
and I am rich enough,
and ask for nothing more.
Amen.

Day Seven: That all Christians will grow in unity so as to one day share the one table of the Lord.

Leader: **In the name of the Father, and of the Son, and of the Holy Spirit.**

All: Amen.

Scripture Reading   Acts 2:42-47 (LFM 977.1)

They devoted themselves to meeting together in the temple area and to breaking bread in their homes.

A reading from the Acts of the Apostles

The brothers and sisters devoted themselves
    to the teaching of the Apostles and to the
        communal life,
    to the breaking of the bread and to the prayers.
Awe came upon everyone,
    and many wonders and signs were done through
        the Apostles.
All who believed were together and had all things in
    common;
    they would sell their property and possessions
    and divide them among all according to each
        one's need.
Every day they devoted themselves
    to meeting together in the temple area
    and to breaking bread in their homes.
They ate their meals with exultation and sincerity
    of heart,
    praising God and enjoying favor with all the people.
And every day the Lord added to their number those
    who were being saved.

The word of the Lord.

Reflection

"The road of ecumenism ultimately points towards a common celebration of the Eucharist (cf. *Ut Unum Sint*, nos. 23-24; 45), which Christ entrusted to his Apostles as the sacrament of the Church's unity *par excellence*. Although there are still obstacles to be overcome, we can be sure that a common Eucharist one day would only strengthen our resolve to love and serve one another in imitation of our Lord: for Jesus' commandment to 'do this in memory of me' (Lk 22:19) is intrinsically ordered to his admonition to 'wash one another's feet' (Jn 13:14). For this reason, a candid dialogue concerning the place of the Eucharist—stimulated by a renewed and attentive study of scripture, patristic writings, and documents from across the two millennia of Christian history (cf. *Ut Unum Sint*, nos. 69-70)—will undoubtedly help to advance the ecumenical movement and unify our witness to the world" (Pope Benedict XVI, Ecumenical meeting in the Crypt of St. Mary's Cathedral in Sydney, Australia, July 18, 2008).

(A time of sacred silence should be observed.)

Leader:

Grant, we pray, almighty God,
that your Church may always remain that holy
**   people,**
formed as one by the unity of Father, Son and
**   Holy Spirit,**
which manifests to the world
the Sacrament of your holiness and unity
and leads it to the perfection of your charity.
Through our Lord Jesus Christ, your Son,
who lives and reigns with you and the Holy Spirit,
one God, forever and ever.

Novena Prayer

Prayer of Self-Offering

Receive, Lord, my entire freedom.
Accept the whole of my memory,
my intellect and my will.
Whatever I have or possess,
it was you who gave it to me;
I restore it to you in full,
and I surrender it completely
to the guidance of your will.
Give me only love of you
together with your grace,
and I am rich enough,
and ask for nothing more.
Amen.

Day Eight: That all the faithful will proclaim the death and resurrection of the Lord through their words and deeds.

Leader: **In the name of the Father, and of the Son, and of the Holy Spirit.**

All: Amen.

Scripture Reading   1 Corinthians 11:23-26 (LFM 979.2)

For as often as you eat the bread and drink the cup, you proclaim the death of the Lord.

A reading from the first Letter of Saint Paul to the Corinthians

Brothers and sisters:
I received from the Lord what I also handed on to you,
     that the Lord Jesus, on the night he was handed over,
     took bread and, after he had given thanks,
     broke it and said, "This is my Body that is for you.
Do this in remembrance of me."
In the same way also the cup, after supper, saying,
     "This cup is the new covenant in my Blood.
Do this, as often as you drink it, in remembrance of me."
For as often as you eat this bread and drink the cup,
     you proclaim the death of the Lord until he comes.

The word of the Lord.

Reflection

"The Eucharist is also Jesus Christ, future, Jesus Christ to come. When we contemplate the sacred host, his glorious transfigured and risen Body, we contemplate what we shall contemplate in eternity, where we shall discover that the whole world has been carried by its Creator during every second of its history. Each time we consume him, but also each time we contemplate him, we proclaim him until he comes again, '*donec veniat*.' That is why we receive him with infinite respect" (Pope Benedict XVI, Meditation during the eucharistic procession in Lourdes, September 14, 2008).

(A time of sacred silence should be observed.)

Leader:

O God, you have willed that your Church
be the sacrament of salvation for all nations
so that Christ's saving work may continue to the
**   end of the ages;**
stir up, we pray, the hearts of your faithful
and grant that they may feel a more urgent call
to work for the salvation of every creature,
so that from all the peoples on earth
one family and one people of your own
may arise and increase.
Through our Lord Jesus Christ, your Son,
who lives and reigns with you and the Holy Spirit,
one God, forever and ever.

Novena Prayer

Prayer of Self-Offering

Receive, Lord, my entire freedom.
Accept the whole of my memory,
my intellect and my will.
Whatever I have or possess,
it was you who gave it to me;
I restore it to you in full,
and I surrender it completely
to the guidance of your will.
Give me only love of you
together with your grace,
and I am rich enough,
and ask for nothing more.
Amen.

Day Nine: That all those who have died in faith may celebrate at the wedding feast of the Lamb.

Leader: **In the name of the Father, and of the Son,**
and of the Holy Spirit.

All: Amen.

Scripture Reading   Revelation 19:1, 5-9a
                                (LFM 802.13)

Blessed are those who have been called to the wedding
feast of the Lamb.

A reading from the Book of Revelation

I, John, heard what sounded like the loud voice
    of a great multitude in heaven, saying:

    "Alleluia!
    Salvation, glory, and might belong to our God."

A voice coming from the throne said:

    "Praise our God, all you his servants,
        and you who revere him, small and great."

Then I heard something like the sound of a great
    multitude
    or the sound of rushing water or mighty peals of
        thunder,
    as they said:
        "Alleluia!
    The Lord has established his reign,
        our God, the almighty.
    Let us rejoice and be glad
        and give him glory.
    For the wedding day of the Lamb has come,
        his bride has made herself ready.
    She was allowed to wear
        a bright, clean linen garment."

(The linen represents the righteous deeds of the holy ones.)

Then the angel said to me,
   "Write this:
   Blessed are those who have been called
   to the wedding feast of the Lamb."

The word of the Lord.

Reflection

"In order to progress on our earthly pilgrimage towards the heavenly Kingdom, we all need to be nourished by the word and the bread of eternal Life, and these are inseparable from one another!" (Pope Benedict XVI, Message for the Twenty-First World Youth Day, February 22, 2006).

(A time of sacred silence should be observed.)

Leader:

**Lord God, whose Son left us,
in the Sacrament of his Body
food for the journey,
mercifully grant that, strengthened by it,
our brother (sister) N. may come
to the eternal table of Christ.**

Who lives and reigns for ever and ever.

Novena Prayer

Prayer of Self-Offering

Receive, Lord, my entire freedom.
Accept the whole of my memory,
my intellect and my will.
Whatever I have or possess,
it was you who gave it to me;
I restore it to you in full,
and I surrender it completely
to the guidance of your will.
Give me only love of you
together with your grace,
and I am rich enough,
and ask for nothing more.
Amen.

APPENDIX D

BULLETIN INSERTS

The United States Conference of Catholic Bishops is offering a series of nine bulletin inserts to help parishes prepare to implement the *Roman Missal, Third Edition*. These bulletin inserts will cover the following topics:

✠ Parts of the Mass
✠ Guide to unfamiliar words in the Mass
✠ Questions about the new *Roman Missal*
✠ Liturgical participation
✠ Praying with body, mind, and voice
✠ Reclaiming the Lord's Day: Celebrating Sunday
✠ Liturgy and life
✠ Questions on dealing with change in the Liturgy
✠ Scripture and the Liturgy

The bulletin inserts are available here in Appendix D and also online at *www.usccb.org/romanmissal*. Parishes and schools have permission to reproduce the bulletin inserts included in this guide or the downloadable PDF versions for free distribution.

Parishes can use these materials in many ways:

✠ Include an insert every week, every two weeks, or every month in the parish bulletin. If you follow a monthly schedule, choose the same Sunday each month (e.g., the first Sunday) so that people will know when to expect the information on the *Roman Missal*.
✠ Use the bulletin inserts as handouts at youth ministry gatherings, RCIA sessions, or meetings of parish groups.
✠ Make the inserts available at sacramental preparation gatherings, including baptismal preparation, marriage preparation, and First Communion meetings.
✠ Send copies home with all students in the parish school or religious education program. Encourage families to discuss the information provided over dinner or during commutes.
✠ Make the inserts available in magazine or brochure racks in the back of the church.
✠ Keep copies of the inserts on hand at the parish office.
✠ Include copies of the inserts with parish mailings.

Parts of the Mass

The Mass follows a "fundamental structure which has been preserved throughout the centuries down to our own day" (*Catechism of the Catholic Church*, no. 1346). Though the Mass is one unified act of worship, it consists of many parts, each with its own purpose and meaning. The entries in this article follow the order in which the parts occur in the Mass.

Introductory Rites: "The rites that precede the Liturgy of the Word, namely, the Entrance, the Greeting, the Penitential Act, the *Kyrie*, the *Glória in excélsis (Glory to God in the highest)* and Collect, have the character of a beginning, an introduction, and a preparation. Their purpose is to ensure that the faithful who come together as one, establish communion and dispose themselves properly to listen to the word of God and to celebrate the Eucharist worthily" (*General Instruction of the Roman Missal* [GIRM], no. 46).

Collect: "The [opening] prayer . . . through which the character of the celebration finds expression" (GIRM, no. 54). This prayer literally "collects" the prayers of all who are gathered into one prayer led by the priest celebrant.

Liturgy of the Word: "The main part of the Liturgy of the Word is made up of the readings from Sacred Scripture together with the chants occurring between them. As for the Homily, the Profession of Faith and the Universal Prayer, they develop and conclude it" (GIRM, no. 55).

Creed: A brief, normative summary statement or profession of Christian faith. The Nicene Creed, which is recited or chanted at Mass, comes from the Councils of Nicea (AD 325) and Constantinople (AD 381).

Canon of the Mass: The central part of the Mass, also known as the Eucharistic Prayer or anaphora, which is the prayer of thanksgiving and consecration. It begins with the Preface Dialogue (i.e., "The Lord be with you. . . . Lift up your hearts. . . . Let us give thanks to the Lord our God") and concludes with a final Doxology ("Through him, and with him, and in him") and Amen.

Epiclesis: The prayer petitioning the Father to send the Holy Spirit to sanctify offerings of bread and wine so that they may become the Body and Blood of Christ.

Consecration: The consecration is that part of the Eucharistic Prayer during which the priest prays the Lord's words of institution of the Eucharist at the Last Supper. Through this prayer the bread and wine become the risen Body and Blood of Jesus.

Anamnesis: From the Greek, meaning "remembrance." We remember Jesus' historical saving deeds in the liturgical action of the Church, which inspires thanksgiving and praise. Every Eucharistic Prayer contains an anamnesis or memorial in which the Church calls to mind the Passion, Resurrection, and glorious return of Christ Jesus.

Doxology: A Christian prayer that gives praise and glory to God often in a special way to the three divine Persons of the Trinity. Liturgical prayers, including the Eucharistic Prayer, traditionally conclude with the Doxology "to the Father, through the Son, in the Holy Spirit."

Communion Rite: The preparatory rites, consisting of the Lord's Prayer, the Rite of Peace, and the Fraction, lead the faithful to Holy Communion (see GIRM, no. 80). The Prayer After Communion expresses the Church's gratitude for the mysteries celebrated and received.

Rite of Peace: The rite "by which the Church asks for peace and unity for herself and for the whole human family, and the faithful express to each other their ecclesial communion and mutual charity before communicating in the Sacrament" (GIRM, no. 82).

Fraction: "The priest breaks the Eucharistic Bread. . . . The gesture of breaking bread done by Christ at the Last Supper . . . in apostolic times gave the entire Eucharistic Action it's name" (GIRM, no. 83).

Communion: Holy Communion, the reception of the Body and Blood of Christ in the Eucharist.

Concluding Rites: "To the Concluding Rites belong the following: brief announcements . . . ; the priest's greeting and blessing . . . ; the dismissal of the people by the deacon or the priest, so that each may go back to doing good works, praising and blessing God; the kissing of the altar by the priest and the deacon, followed by a profound bow to the altar by the priest, the deacon, and the other ministers" (GIRM, no. 90).

REFERENCES

Catechism of the Catholic Church (2nd ed.). Washington, DC: United States Conference of Catholic Bishops (USCCB), 2000.

General Instruction of the Roman Missal. Liturgy Documentary Series 2. Washington, DC: USCCB, 2003.

This page is blank for reproduction purposes.

Words in the *Roman Missal, Third Edition*

Some of the words used in the new translation of the Mass may be unfamiliar to some Catholics. The following list of definitions may help to increase your understanding of the rich theology that underlies these texts.

Abasement: The lowering of one of higher rank. Jesus abased himself in that, though he was God, he lowered himself and became a human being so that he might save us from our sins (see Phil 2:6-11).

Adoption: In Baptism, the Holy Spirit transforms us into children of the Father, thereby making us his adopted sons and daughters in the likeness of his eternal Son (see Eph 1:3-6). In this way, the faithful are made "partakers in the divine nature (cf. 2 Pt 1:4) by uniting them in a living union with the only Son, the Savior" (*Catechism of the Catholic Church* [CCC], no. 1129). In the sacraments, we become the sons and daughters of God by adoption through Christ Jesus.

Angels and archangels, cherubim and seraphim, thrones and dominions: Spiritual, personal, and immortal creatures, with intelligence and free will, who glorify God and serve him as messengers of his saving plan. Traditionally, the choirs of angels have been divided into various ranks, including archangels, cherubim, seraphim, thrones, dominions, principalities, and powers (see Col 1:16).

Chalice: From the Latin word "calix" meaning "cup" (see Ps 116:13; Mt 20:22; 1 Cor 10:16). The use of this term in the Liturgy points to the chalice's function as a particular kind of cup and indicates the uniqueness of what it contains, the very Blood of Christ.

Clemency: The loving kindness, compassion, or mercy that God shows to sinners.

Communion: Our fellowship and union with Jesus and other baptized Christians in the Church, which has its source and summit in the celebration of the Eucharist. By receiving Jesus in Holy Communion, we are united to him and one another as members of his Body.

Consecration: The dedication of a thing or person to divine service by a prayer or blessing. In the Mass, "consecration" also refers to the words spoken by the priest whereby the bread and wine are transformed into the risen Body and Blood of Jesus.

Consubstantial: The belief, articulated in the Nicene Creed, about the relationship of the Father and the Son: that "in the Father and with the Father, the Son is one and the same God" (CCC, no. 262).

Contrite: To be repentant within one's heart and mind for sins committed and to resolve not to sin again.

Covenant: A solemn agreement between human beings, between God and a human being, or between God and a people involving mutual commitments or promises. In the Old Testament, God made a covenant with the Jewish people. Jesus, through his death and Resurrection, made a new covenant with the whole of humanity. One enters into this new covenant through faith and Baptism.

Damnation: Eternal separation from God's love caused by dying in mortal sin without repentance.

Godhead: The mystery of one God in three Persons: Father, Son, and Holy Spirit.

Homage: The honor, respect, and reverence due to another. Homage is especially due to God, for he is eternal, all good, all holy, and all loving.

Implore: To plead, beseech, or ask with humility. This is an example of the self-deprecatory language in the *Roman Missal* that helps to express our dependence on God. We humbly beg the Father to hear and answer our prayers, for we ask them in the power of the Holy Spirit and in the name of Jesus.

Incarnation: The Son of God assumed human nature and became man by being conceived by the Holy Spirit in the womb of the Virgin Mary. Jesus is true God and true man. As man, the Son of God obtained our salvation. The use of this term in the Nicene Creed indicates that Jesus' birth has a significance beyond that of any other human birth.

Ineffable: That which cannot be conceived or expressed fully (see 1 Cor 2:6-9). One cannot, for example, adequately describe in concepts and words the mystery of the Trinity or the mystery of the Incarnation.

Infusion: The Holy Spirit is poured into the hearts and souls of believers, and so they are filled, or infused, with grace.

Intercessor: One who makes a petition on behalf of others. Our unique intercessor is Jesus Christ, who intercedes on our behalf with the Father (see Rom 8:34). The priest at Mass acting in the person of Christ intercedes on behalf of the whole Church.

Justification: The gracious action by which God frees us from sin and makes us holy and righteous before him.

Lord, God of Hosts: From the word "sabaoth," hosts are the invisible powers that work at God's command over heaven and earth.

Mediator: One who unites or reconciles separate or opposing parties. Thus, Jesus Christ is the "one mediator between God and the human race" (1 Tm 2:5). Through his sacrificial offering he has become high priest and unique mediator who has gained for us access to the Father through the Holy Spirit.

Merit: The reward that God promises and gives to those who love him and who by his grace perform good works. One cannot earn justification or eternal life; they are the free gifts of God. Rather our merit is from God through Christ in the Holy Spirit. The Father freely justifies us in Christ through the indwelling of the Spirit; and Christians, by the same Holy Spirit, are empowered to do good works of love and justice. In cooperating with the Holy Spirit, the faithful receive further grace and thus, in Christ, cooperate in the work of their salvation.

Oblation: A gift or sacrifice offered to God.

Only-Begotten Son: This title "signifies the unique and eternal relationship of Jesus Christ to God his Father: he is the only Son of the Father (cf. Jn 1:14, 18; 3:16, 18); he is God himself (cf. Jn 1:1)" (CCC, no. 454). Jesus is the Son of God not by adoption but by nature.

Paschal: Referring to Christ's work of redemption accomplished through his Passion, death, Resurrection, and Ascension. Through the Paschal Mystery, Jesus destroyed our death and restored us to life. The Paschal Mystery is celebrated and made present in the Liturgy so that we can obtain the fruit of Jesus' death and Resurrection, that is, the forgiveness of our sins and the new life of the Holy Spirit.

Patriarchs: Title given to the venerable ancestors or "fathers" of the Semitic peoples, Abraham, Isaac, and Jacob, who received God's promise of election.

Precursor: One who comes before as a herald. John the Baptist is the precursor of Jesus.

Provident grace: The free and undeserved gift that God gives us as he protects and governs all creation.

Redemption: Jesus Christ is our Savior and Redeemer because he frees us from our sin through his sacrificial death on the Cross.

Temporal: What pertains to this world of time and history, as opposed to what pertains to God, such as our new life in Christ through the indwelling of the Holy Spirit.

Venerate: To show devotion and respect to holy things and people. Catholics venerate relics and saints. Veneration must be clearly distinguished from adoration and worship, both of which pertain solely to the Trinity and Jesus as the Son of God.

REFERENCES

Catechism of the Catholic Church (2nd ed.). Washington, DC: United States Conference of Catholic Bishops, 2000.

General Instruction of the Roman Missal. Liturgy Documentary Series 2. Washington, DC: United States Conference of Catholic Bishops, 2003.

Ten Questions on the
Roman Missal, Third Edition

1. Why is there a need for a new translation?

Pope John Paul II issued the third edition of the *Missale Romanum* (the Latin text of the *Roman Missal*) during the Jubilee Year in 2000. This new edition included many new texts requiring translation. In addition, the experience of the years after the Second Vatican Council gave rise to a desire for more formal and literal translations of the original Latin texts. This new translation will employ the best of what we have learned about translation and liturgical language in two generations of celebrating the Liturgy in the vernacular. It will provide an opportunity to reflect ever more deeply on the eucharistic celebration that lies at the heart of the Church's life.

2. Who is doing the work of translation?

The process of translating liturgical texts from the original Latin is a highly consultative work done by several groups. The International Commission on English in the Liturgy (ICEL) prepares English translations of liturgical texts on behalf of the conferences of bishops of English-speaking countries. The United States Conference of Catholic Bishops (USCCB) and the other member conferences receive draft translations of each text and have the opportunity to offer comments and suggestions to ICEL. Then ICEL proposes a second draft, which each conference approves and submits to the Vatican for final approval. Each conference reserves the right to amend or modify a particular text.

At the Vatican, the Congregation for Divine Worship and the Discipline of the Sacraments examines the translated texts, offers authoritative approval (*recognitio*) of the texts, and grants permission for their use. Currently the Congregation is aided by the recommendations of Vox Clara, a special committee of bishops and consultants from English-speaking countries. The translation and review process is guided by the guidelines in *Liturgiam Authenticam*, issued in 2001, an instruction from the Congregation that outlines the principles and rules for liturgical translation. In 2007, the Congregation also issued a *ratio* outlining the specific rules for translation in English.

3. What's new or different about the revised translation?

The style of the translation of the third edition is different. In accord with the rules for translation established by the Holy See, the revised translation follows the style of the original Latin texts more closely, including concrete images, repetition, parallelisms, and rhythm. The English used in the Mass texts is more formal and dignified in style. Where possible, the texts follow the language of Scripture and include many poetic images.

In addition, the third edition contains prayers for the celebration of recently canonized saints, additional prefaces for the Eucharistic Prayers, additional Masses and prayers for various needs and intentions, and some updated and revised rubrics (or instructions) for the celebration of the Mass.

4. What is the timeline for the approval and implementation of the *Missal*?

After the Latin *Missale Romanum* was published in 2002, ICEL began its work of preparing a draft English translation of the text. ICEL presented the first section—the Order of Mass, which contains the fixed prayers of the Mass, including the people's parts—to the English-speaking conferences of bishops in 2004. The USCCB approved the final version in 2006, and the Holy See confirmed this section in June 2008. The remaining sections were approved between 2007 and 2009. The USCCB completed its approval of the *Missal* in November 2009. The Holy See granted the final approval of the text in the spring of 2010. Cardinal Francis George, OMI, president of the USCCB, announced that parishes may begin using the revised translation on November 27, 2011.

5. Can we start using the texts approved by the bishops immediately?

The translation of the *Missale Romanum* could not be used in the celebration of the Mass until the complete text was confirmed by the Holy See. Now that the translation has received the *recognitio*, the USCCB has established the first day on which the new translation may be used. Use of the revised text requires preparation and catechesis for both priests and the faithful. When the time comes to use the texts in the celebration of the Mass, priests will be properly trained, the faithful will have an understanding and appreciation of what is being prayed, and musical settings for the liturgical texts will be readily available.

6. What will the process of implementation look like?

Now that the *recognitio* has been granted, final preparation and publication of the *Missal* will commence. Catechesis on the new translation and on the Liturgy itself will become even more important. Training for priests, music ministers, and other liturgical leaders (liturgy committees and liturgical commissions), as well as formation for all Catholics, will help to ensure the successful implementation of the new text.

7. What will the new *Missal* mean in my parish?

In the months before the revised translation is implemented, parishes will have to do many things. The parish will have to replace liturgical books and participation aids. Priests will practice proclaiming the new texts and will prepare homilies helping the faithful to understand the new translation and to deepen their appreciation for the Liturgy. The music ministers and the people will learn new musical settings for the parts of the Mass (such as the *Gloria* and the *Sanctus*). Catechists and teachers will help parishioners learn the new prayers. Parishes may also use this opportunity to undertake a thorough reexamination of their liturgical practices.

8. If my parish likes the old translation better, can we continue using that one?

Now that the Holy See has granted the *recognitio* to the revised translation, the USCCB has established a date for first use and a date for mandatory use. No parish may continue to use the current translation after the mandatory use date. Parishes will need to use the period before the mandatory use date to help parishioners renew their love for the Sacred Liturgy, to understand the changes, and to develop an appreciation for the revised translation.

9. Do these changes mean that the old translation was not valid and orthodox?

The current translation was approved by the conferences of bishops and confirmed by the Holy See. Until the new text becomes effective, the current translation remains the valid ordinary form of the Liturgy in the Roman Rite. The revised translation attempts to address some inadequacies in the present translation by introducing a more elevated style of language and by retaining many poetic texts and scriptural allusions. The current translation fostered the faith of two generations of Catholics and retains a valid place in church history.

10. What opportunities does the new *Missal* offer the Church?

Implementing the new *Missal* will give the Church an opportunity to take a fresh look at its liturgical practice and to renew its celebration of the Sacred Liturgy, which is the "source and summit" of Christian life (Second Vatican Council, *Dogmatic Constitution on the Church* [*Lumen Gentium*], no. 11). The faithful, encountering the Liturgy anew in the new text, can deepen their sharing in Christ's sacrifice, offering their lives to the Father as they worship "in Spirit and truth" (Jn 4:23).

REFERENCE

Second Vatican Council. *Dogmatic Constitution on the Church* (*Lumen Gentium*). In *Vatican Council II: Volume I: The Conciliar and Post Conciliar Documents* (new rev. ed.), edited by Austin Flannery. Northport, NY: Costello Publishing, 1996.

The celebration of Mass is an act of the whole assembly gathered for worship. In the Mass, the Church is joined to the action of Christ. We are joined to this divine action through Baptism, which incorporates us into the risen Christ. This action, which lies at "the center of the whole of Christian life" (*General Instruction of the Roman Missal* [GIRM], no. 16), is initiated not by us but by God acting in and through the Church as the Body of the risen Christ. The Liturgy is designed to bring about in all those who make up the worshiping assembly a "participation of the faithful, namely in body and in mind, a participation fervent with faith, hope, and charity" (GIRM, no. 18). To the extent that we are able to participate in this way, the work of redemption becomes personally effective for each of us. By such participation we make the actions and prayers of the Liturgy our own; we enter more fully into our personal communion with Christ's redeeming act and perfect worship.

"In the celebration of Mass the faithful form a holy people, a people of God's own possession and a royal priesthood, so that they may give thanks to God and offer the unblemished sacrificial Victim not only by means of the hands of the priest but also together with him, and so that they map learn to offer their very selves. They should, moreover, take care to show this by their deep religious sense and their charity toward brothers and sisters who participate with them in the same celebration. . . . Moreover, they are to form one body, whether in hearing the word of God, or in taking part in the prayers and in the singing, or above all by the common offering of the Sacrifice and by a participating together at the Lord's table" (GIRM, nos. 95, 96).

The participation of each person in the Liturgy is important. Each person needs to do his or her part.

ORDAINED MINISTRIES IN THE LITURGY

Bishops and priests are called to act in the Liturgy in the very person of Christ, on behalf of his people, pronouncing the most sacred prayers of our faith, presiding over the celebration of the sacred mysteries, explaining God's Word and feeding God's People on the Body and Blood of Christ. A bishop has the added responsibility of being the chief shepherd, the principal liturgist of his diocese in his role as the successor of the Apostles. By God's grace others are ordained to the ministry of deacon. In the celebration of the Mass deacons proclaim the Gospel, occasionally preach the homily, and assist the bishop and priest in exercising their sacred duties.

OTHER LITURGICAL MINISTRIES

In addition to the ordained ministries, some roles in the Liturgy are exercised by lay people who place their time and talent at the service of the liturgical assembly as acolytes (altar servers), lectors, extraordinary ministers of Holy Communion, cantors, choir members, instrumentalists, leaders of song, and ushers. Others contribute their time and talent to planning and organizing the Liturgy; to keeping the church and the vestments, vessels, and appointments clean and well ordered; or to providing decorations that reflect the spirit of the liturgical feast or season.

This variety of offices and roles is desirable and should be maintained. It is desirable that individuals function in roles of service at Mass. For example, if a deacon is present, the priest celebrant or a concelebrant should not read the Gospel. The lector should not take on the role of a server or an extraordinary minister of Holy Communion. A wide variety of services needs to be performed, and it is preferable that different individuals exercise those services so that the talents and gifts God has placed within the Christian community are fully used and that these roles of service are not monopolized by a few.

Those engaged in liturgical roles need to be well prepared for those roles and to know how to carry them out with reverence, dignity, and understanding. Receiving the proper preparation requires a further gift of time on the part of the person being prepared as well as on the part of those in the parish responsible for the training of liturgical ministers. Finally, the practical task of assigning individuals to particular Masses and organizing the distribution of roles is another indispensable element in the fabric of well-ordered liturgical ministry in a parish.

All the baptized need to understand that part of their duty regarding the Liturgy is to accept some responsibility for the Liturgy, to place themselves and their God-given talents at the service of the liturgical community whenever possible. Whether one brings up the gifts at the Presentation; reads the Word of God; assists with the distribution of Communion and brings the Eucharist to those unable to be present at Mass; serves at the altar; provides music that augments the joy, solemnity, and festivity of the celebration; or serves the assembled community as an usher, he or she is contributing to the worship of the community and fulfilling the responsibility that comes with Baptism.

Not all members of the parish community will have the time, energy, strength, or ability to serve in these roles. However, individuals must be careful not to excuse themselves too easily. What is important is that all understand that the celebration of Liturgy is not just the responsibility of the pastor, although he is delegated by the bishop to oversee the liturgical life of the parish. Pastors need the help of people who are serious about living out their baptismal right and responsibility to worship.

THE ROLE OF THE BAPTIZED

This catalog of specialized roles might give the impression that those who are not exercising one of these roles are free to sit back passively and simply let the Liturgy happen around them. Nothing could be further from the truth. Those who come together for Liturgy do not have the luxury of acting as spectators, waiting for all to be done for them. "Full, conscious, and active participation" in the Liturgy (as commended by the Second Vatican Council) is not only their right but also their duty and their responsibility. That responsibility includes full engagement throughout the liturgical celebration. The baptized faithful who form the congregation are called to join in praise and thanksgiving in song and spoken word, to listen attentively to God's Word, and to exercise their baptismal priesthood in prayer for the Church, the world, and all in need during the General Intercessions.

In the Liturgy of the Eucharist the baptized faithful join their prayer to that of the priest celebrant, offering Christ the Victim, "not only by means of the hands of the priest but also together with him," and offer themselves as well (GIRM, no. 95). Their participation culminates in the reception of the Body and Blood of the Lord, the sacrament that unites them more fully with Christ their Head and with one another. We need to be aware, therefore, that "participation" does not refer primarily to external activity or function during the celebration of Mass; rather, it refers to a deeply spiritual, interior participation of mind and heart, filled with devotion and penetrating the very depths of the mysteries we celebrate.

In their sincere efforts to participate, those present minister to the priest celebrant, to others who serve in liturgical roles, and to one another. Their attention and active engagement in the celebration can draw from the priest celebrant and the other ministers the best they have to offer. Their enthusiastic song and verbal responses made with conviction can encourage others to sing and respond; their very presence at the celebration of Mass when so many other enticing options might have been chosen instead supports and reinforces others who have made the same choice.

The Liturgy, then, is about the action of God's own people, each with different offices and roles. When we play our roles in the Liturgy with our bodies, minds, and hearts fully engaged, we make to God a perfect sacrifice of praise.

REFERENCES

General Instruction of the Roman Missal. Liturgy Documentary Series 2. Washington, DC: United States Conference of Catholic Bishops, 2003.

Second Vatican Council. *Constitution on the Sacred Liturgy (Sacrosanctum Concilium).* In *Vatican Council II: Volume I: The Conciliar and Post Conciliar Documents* (new rev. ed.), edited by Austin Flannery. Northport, NY: Costello Publishing, 1996.

In the celebration of Mass we raise our hearts and minds to God. We are creatures of body as well as spirit, so our prayer is not confined to our minds and hearts. It is expressed by our bodies as well. When our bodies are engaged in our prayer, we pray with our whole person. Using our entire being in prayer helps us to pray with greater attentiveness.

During Mass we assume different postures—standing, kneeling, sitting—and we are also invited to make a variety of gestures. These postures and gestures are not merely ceremonial. They have profound meaning and, when done with understanding, can enhance our participation in the Mass.

STANDING

Standing is a sign of respect and honor, so we stand as the celebrant who represents Christ enters and leaves the assembly. From the earliest days of the Church, this posture has been understood as the stance of those who have risen with Christ and seek the things that are above. When we stand for prayer, we assume our full stature before God, not in pride but in humble gratitude for the marvelous things God has done in creating and redeeming each one of us. By Baptism we have been given a share in the life of God, and the posture of standing is an acknowledgment of this wonderful gift. We stand for the proclamation of the Gospel, which recounts the words and deeds of the Lord. The bishops of the United States have chosen standing as the posture to be observed for the reception of Communion.

KNEELING

In the early Church, kneeling signified penance. So thoroughly was kneeling identified with penance that the early Christians were forbidden to kneel on Sundays and during the Easter season, when the prevailing spirit of the Liturgy was one of joy and thanksgiving. In the Middle Ages kneeling came to signify homage, and more recently this posture has come to signify adoration, especially before the presence of Christ in the Eucharist. It is for this reason that the bishops of this country have chosen the posture of kneeling for the entire Eucharistic Prayer.

SITTING

Sitting is the posture of listening and meditation, so the congregation sits for the pre-Gospel readings and the homily and may also sit for the period of meditation following Communion. All should strive to assume a seated posture during the Mass that is attentive rather than merely at rest.

PROCESSIONS

Every procession in the Liturgy is a sign of the pilgrim Church, the body of those who believe in Christ, on their way to the Heavenly Jerusalem. The Mass begins with the procession of the priest and ministers to the altar. The Book of the Gospels is carried in procession to the ambo. The gifts of bread and wine are brought forward to the altar. Members of the assembly come forward in procession—eagerly, attentively, and devoutly—to receive Holy Communion. We who believe in Christ are moving in time toward that moment when we will leave this world and enter into the joy of the Lord in the eternal Kingdom he has prepared for us.

MAKING THE SIGN OF THE CROSS

We begin and end Mass by marking ourselves with the Sign of the Cross. Because it was by his death on the Cross that Christ redeemed humankind, we trace the Sign of the Cross on our foreheads, lips, and hearts at the beginning of the Gospel, praying that the Word of God may be always in our minds, on our lips, and in our hearts. The cross reminds us in a physical way of the Paschal Mystery we celebrate: the death and Resurrection of our Savior Jesus Christ.

BOWING

Bowing signifies reverence, respect, and gratitude. In the Creed we bow at the words that commemorate the Incarnation. We also bow as a sign of reverence before we receive Communion. The priest and other ministers bow to the altar, a symbol of Christ, when entering or leaving the sanctuary. As a sign of respect and reverence even in our speech, we bow our heads at the name of Jesus, at the mention of the Three Persons of the Trinity, at the name of the Blessed Virgin Mary, and at the name of the saint whose particular feast or memorial is being observed (see GIRM, no. 275).

GENUFLECTING

As a sign of adoration, we genuflect by bringing our right knee to the floor. Many people also make the Sign of the Cross as they bend their knee. Traditionally, Catholics genuflect on entering and leaving church if the Blessed Sacrament is present in the sanctuary of the Church. The priest and deacon genuflect to the tabernacle on entering and leaving the sanctuary. The priest also genuflects in adoration after he shows the Body and Blood of Christ to the people after the consecration and again before inviting the people to Holy Communion.

ORANS

The priest frequently uses this ancient prayer posture, extending his hands to his sides, slightly elevated. *Orans* means "praying." Early Christian art frequently depicts the saints and others standing in this posture, offering their prayers and surrendering themselves, with hands uplifted to the Lord, in a gesture that echoes Christ's outstretched arms as he offered himself on the Cross.

PROSTRATING

In this rarely used posture, an individual lays full-length on the floor, face to the ground. A posture of deep humility, it signifies our willingness to share in Christ's death so as to share in his Resurrection (see Rom 6). It is used at the beginning of the Celebration of the Lord's Passion on Good Friday and also during the Litany of the Saints in the Rite of Ordination, when those to be ordained deacons, priests, and bishops prostrate themselves in humble prayer and submission to Christ.

SINGING

"By its very nature song has both an individual and a communal dimension. Thus, it is no wonder that singing together in church expresses so well the sacramental presence of God to his people" (United States Conference of Catholic Bishops, *Sing to the Lord*, no. 2). As we raise our voices as one in the prayers, dialogues, and chants of the Mass, most especially in the Eucharistic

Prayer, as well as the other hymns and songs, we each lend our individual voices to the great hymn of praise and thanksgiving to the Triune God.

PRAYING IN UNISON

In the Mass, the worshiping assembly prays in one voice, speaking or singing together the words of the prayers. By saying the same words at the same time, we act as what we truly are—one Body united in Christ through the Sacrament of Baptism.

BEING SILENT

"Silence in the Liturgy allows the community to reflect on what it has heard and experienced, and to open its heart to the mystery celebrated" (*Sing to the Lord*, no. 118). We gather in silence, taking time to separate ourselves from the concerns of the world and enter into the sacred action. We reflect on the readings in silence. We may take time for silent reflection and prayer after Holy Communion. These times of silence are not merely times when nothing happens; rather, they are opportunities for us to enter more deeply in what God is doing in the Mass, and, like Mary, to keep "all these things, reflecting on them" in our hearts (Lk 2:19).

CONCLUSION

The Church sees in these common postures and gestures both a symbol of the unity of those who have come together to worship and also a means of fostering that unity. We are not free to change these postures to suit our own individual piety, for the Church makes it clear that our unity of posture and gesture is an expression of our participation in the one Body formed by the baptized with Christ, our head. When we stand, kneel, sit, bow, and sign ourselves in common action, we give unambiguous witness that we are indeed the Body of Christ, united in body, mind, and voice.

REFERENCE

United States Conference of Catholic Bishops (USCCB). *Sing to the Lord: Music in Divine Worship*. Pastoral Liturgy Series 4. Washington, DC: USCCB, 2007.

Celebrating the Lord's Day

On Sunday, we gather as the Body of Christ to celebrate the Lord's Day, the day of Christ's Resurrection:

> As "the first day of the week" (Mk 16:2) it recalls the first creation; and as the "eighth day," which follows the sabbath, it symbolizes the new creation ushered in by the Resurrection of Christ. Thus, it has become for Christians the first of all days and of all feasts. It is the *day of the Lord* in which he with his Passover fulfilled the spiritual truth of the Jewish Sabbath and proclaimed man's eternal rest in God. (*Compendium of the Catechism of the Catholic Church*, no. 452)

The Scriptures tell us that Jesus rose on the first day of the week—the day following the Jewish Sabbath. Shortly after daybreak, the women found the tomb empty and Jesus risen from the dead. Jesus' death and Resurrection opened for us the doors of salvation. Sharing in Jesus' death in Baptism, we hope to share in his Resurrection. We become a new creation in Christ. It is that new creation which we celebrate on Sunday:

> This is the day the LORD has made;
> let us rejoice in it and be glad. (Ps 118:24)

Each Sunday is a "little Easter"—a celebration of the central mysteries of our faith.

THE SUNDAY EUCHARIST

The primary way in which we celebrate the Lord's Day is with our participation in the Sunday Eucharist. What better way to celebrate the Resurrection of the Lord than by celebration of the memorial of his Passion, death, and Resurrection?

This celebration is not a solitary, private event. Instead, we come together as the People of God, the Church, to worship with one heart and one voice. The *Catechism of the Catholic Church* (CCC) teaches that "participation in the communal celebration of the Sunday Eucharist is a testimony of belonging and of being faithful to Christ and to his Church" (CCC, no. 2182).

When members of our church community are absent from this gathering, they are missed. No member of the faithful should be absent from the Sunday Eucharist without a serious reason. The Liturgy should be the first thing on Sunday's schedule, not the last. We should arrive on time, prepared in mind and heart to fully participate in the Mass. Those who cannot attend because of illness or the need to care for infants or the sick deserve our prayers and special attention.

Often, people will suggest that going to Sunday Mass is not necessary. After all, they can pray at home just as well. This has clearly been an issue in the Church for more than a millennium. In the fourth century, St. John Chrysostom addressed this problem directly:

> You cannot pray at home as at church, where there is a great multitude, where exclamations are cried out to God as from one great heart, and where there is something more: the union of minds, the accord of souls, the bond of charity, the prayers of the priests. (CCC, no. 2179, quoting St. John Chrysostom, *De incomprehensibili* 3, 6: PG 48, 725)

Private prayer, though essential to the spiritual life, can never replace the celebration of the eucharistic Liturgy and the reception of Holy Communion.

In some communities, the lack of priests makes it impossible to celebrate the Eucharist each Sunday. In such instances, the bishop may make provision for these parish communities to gather and celebrate the Liturgy of the Word or the Liturgy of the Hours. These Sunday celebrations in the absence of a priest may or may not include the reception of Holy Communion. Still, these celebrations allow the People of God to gather and keep holy the Lord's Day.

KEEPING SUNDAY—ALL DAY

Celebrating the Sunday Eucharist—though central and essential—does not complete our observance of Sunday. In addition to attending Mass each Sunday, we should also refrain "from those activities which impede the worship of God and disturb the joy proper to the day of the Lord or the necessary relaxation of mind and body" (*Compendium of the Catechism of the Catholic Church*, no. 453).

Sunday has traditionally been a day of rest. However, the concept of a day of rest may seem odd in a world that runs 24/7, where we are tethered to our jobs by a variety of electronic gadgets, where businesses run as normal no matter what the day of the week, and where silence seems to be an endangered species. By taking a day each week to rest in the Lord, we provide a living example to the culture that all time belongs to God and that people are more important than things.

As Pope John Paul II said in *Dies Domini* (*The Day of the Lord*), his apostolic letter on Sunday:

> Through Sunday rest, daily concerns and tasks can find their proper perspective: the material things about which we worry give way to spiritual values; in a moment of encounter and less pressured exchange, we see the true face of the people with whom we live. Even the beauties of nature—too often marred by the desire to exploit, which turns against man himself—can be rediscovered and enjoyed to the full. (*Dies Domini*, no. 67)

Not everyone has the freedom to take Sundays away from work. Some people, including medical professionals and public safety workers, must work on Sundays to keep the rest of us safe and healthy. Others must work for economic reasons beyond their control.

Resting on Sunday does not mean that we are inactive. Instead,

> Sunday is traditionally consecrated by Christian piety to good works and humble service of the sick, the infirm, and the elderly. Christians will also sanctify Sunday by devoting time and care to their families and relatives, often difficult to do on other days of the week. Sunday is a time for reflection, silence, cultivation of the mind, and meditation which furthers the growth of the Christian interior life. (CCC, no. 2186)

To celebrate the Lord's Day more fully, consider trying the following:

- ✠ Don't use Sunday as your catch-all day for errands and household chores.
- ✠ Share a family dinner after Mass. Have the whole family join in the preparation and cleanup.
- ✠ Go for a walk or bike ride and give thanks to God for the beauty of nature.
- ✠ Spend time reading the Bible or a spiritual book.
- ✠ Pray the Rosary or the Liturgy of the Hours, alone or with others.
- ✠ Volunteer in a local food pantry.
- ✠ Visit parishioners and others who are homebound.
- ✠ Read Bible stories to your children.
- ✠ Turn off your gadgets and enjoy the silence.

As we take time each week to celebrate the Paschal Mystery in the Eucharist and to rest from the burdens of our daily lives, we remind ourselves that we are made in the image and likeness of God who "rested on the seventh day from all the work he had undertaken" (Gn 2:2).

REFERENCES

Catechism of the Catholic Church (2nd ed.). Washington, DC: United States Conference of Catholic Bishops, 2000.

Compendium of the Catechism of the Catholic Church. Washington, DC: United States Conference of Catholic Bishops, 2006.

Pope John Paul II, *On Keeping the Lord's Day Holy* (*Dies Domini*). www.vatican.va/holy_father/john_paul_ii/apost_letters/documents/hf_jp-ii_apl_05071998_dies-domini_en.html.

At its heart, the Eucharist is a sacrament of communion, bringing us closer to God and to our brothers and sisters in the Body of Christ. If we live the fruits of the Eucharist in our daily lives, we will fill our families and our communities with the life-giving qualities that the Liturgy brings: hospitality, concern for the poor and vulnerable, self-offering, and thanksgiving.

An ancient saying in the Church reads "*lex orandi, lex credendi*," meaning that the law of prayer is the law of faith. More loosely: as we pray, so we believe. To that we might add *lex vivendi*, meaning that as we pray, so we believe, and so we live. In the third edition of the *Roman Missal*, the bishops and translators have taken great care to ensure that the prayers accurately and fully reflect the mysteries of our faith. Thus, the words that we pray in each liturgical celebration will help to form and strengthen our understanding of the faith.

However, if the effects of the Liturgy stop at the doors of the church, we have not made our prayer and our faith part of our law of living. The *Catechism of the Catholic Church* (CCC) teaches that the Eucharist helps us to grow in union with Christ, avoid sin, increase in charity, strengthen communion with our brothers and sisters, and recognize Christ in the poorest and most vulnerable members of society (see CCC, nos. 1391-1397). But what does that mean in daily life?

LIVING A LIFE OF PRAYER

Our prayer lives should not be limited to a single hour on Sunday mornings. In fact, the richer our prayer lives are throughout the week, the more fully we will be able to enter into the Sunday celebration of the Eucharist. Here are some ways to make your daily life more prayerful:

✠ Try attending daily Mass at least once a week. Your parish may have an early morning Mass, or a church near your job may offer a lunchtime Mass.

✠ Stop in a church before or after work or on your lunch hour for fifteen minutes of quiet prayer before the Blessed Sacrament.

✠ Make it a practice to say grace before every meal—even if you are eating in the car.

✠ Schedule time for family prayer at least once a week. This prayer can be as simple as saying the Our Father or a decade of the Rosary together.

✠ Take time during the week to read or listen to the readings for the upcoming Sunday. The readings are available online (in print and audio) at *www.usccb.org/nab*.

✠ Begin your day with a brief prayer of thanksgiving to God, offering your day to him.

✠ End your day with an examination of conscience, looking at your successes and failures in what you have done or what you have failed to do. If you are aware of serious sin, receive the Sacrament of Penance before you receive Holy Communion again.

LIVING A LIFE OF LOVING SERVICE

Celebrating the eucharistic Liturgy and receiving Holy Communion should strengthen us to conform our lives more closely to the example of Christ. As Jesus knelt before his Apostles to wash their feet (see Jn 13), giving them an example of humble service, so must we who bear the name Christian live our lives in service to our brothers and sisters.

To help us in this endeavor, Church Tradition has identified works of mercy. These fourteen practices demand great sacrifice and generosity, but they also draw us more deeply into conformity with the Lord. Focusing on one of these works each week may be a practical way to integrate them into our personal, family, and parish lives.

Corporal Works of Mercy

✠ Feeding the hungry
✠ Sheltering the homeless
✠ Clothing the naked
✠ Visiting the sick
✠ Visiting the imprisoned
✠ Giving drink to the thirsty
✠ Burying the dead

Spiritual Works of Mercy

- ✠ Converting sinners
- ✠ Instructing the ignorant
- ✠ Advising the doubtful
- ✠ Comforting the sorrowful
- ✠ Bearing wrongs patiently
- ✠ Forgiving injuries
- ✠ Praying for the living and dead

Our parishes and civil communities offer numerous opportunities to live out these works, from assisting with religious education classes or volunteering at a food bank to encouraging our legislators to put forward policies that protect the life and dignity of each person. As we grow in conformity to Christ, we see more clearly that all people are made in the image and likeness of God (see Gn 1:26) and so have an inherent value and dignity. By helping to build a more just and compassionate society, we act as Christ's Body in the world.

IT ALL COMES BACK TO THE EUCHARIST

Living the Christian life is not easy. "What material food produces in our bodily life, Holy Communion wonderfully achieves in our spiritual life. Communion with the flesh of the risen Christ . . . preserves, increases, and renews the life of grace received at Baptism. This growth in Christian life needs the nourishment of Eucharistic Communion, the bread for our pilgrimage" (CCC, no. 1392).

And so, each Sunday, we return to the eucharistic table, bringing all our efforts of the previous week, the good and the bad, the successes and the failures, the joys and the sorrows. We gather with our brothers and sisters in the Lord and, together with our priest, we join these efforts to the perfect sacrifice of Christ, asking that God will receive what we offer back to him in humble thanksgiving. The *Catechism* explains it as follows:

> The Church which is the Body of Christ participates in the offering of her Head. With him, she herself is offered whole and entire. She unites herself to his intercession with the Father for all men. In the Eucharist the sacrifice of Christ becomes also the sacrifice of the members of his Body. The lives of the faithful, their praise, sufferings, prayer, and work, are united with those of Christ and with his total offering, and so acquire a new value. Christ's sacrifice present on the altar makes it possible for all generations of Christians to be united with his offering. (CCC, no. 1368)

Then, strengthened by Holy Communion, we are once again sent forth into the world to glorify the Lord in our lives.

REFERENCE

Catechism of the Catholic Church (2nd ed.). Washington, DC: United States Conference of Catholic Bishops, 2000.

For many people, change does not come easy. Change requires us to stop doing things a certain way in order to do something else. Many people find comfort in familiar routines and known ways of acting. Change interrupts those familiar routines. But change is also an opportunity to stop and reflect on what we are doing and to come to a better understanding of God, who does not change.

Why does the Church change the Liturgy?

In its Liturgy, the Church always attempts to follow the "norm of the holy Fathers." This effort "requires not only the preservation of what our immediate forebears have handed on to us, but also an understanding and a more profound pondering of the Church's entire past. . . . this broader view allows us to see how the Holy Spirit endows the People of God with a marvelous fidelity in preserving the unalterable deposit of faith, even though there is a very great variety of prayers and rites" (*General Instruction of the Roman Missal*, no. 9).

The Liturgy must, therefore, always celebrate and make present the Paschal Sacrifice of Christ—his saving Passion, death, Resurrection, and Ascension. However, over time, it may become necessary to make certain changes, such as adding prayers for recently canonized saints and adding texts that reflect the needs that the People of God wish to bring to God in prayer. The third edition of the *Roman Missal* makes such additions and provides a fresh translation of the Latin texts of the existing content of the *Missal*.

Who decides that the Liturgy should change?

Pope John Paul II approved the promulgation of the third edition of the *Missale Romanum*, the Latin text, on April 20, 2000. The final Latin edition of the revised text was published in March 2002. The Congregation for Divine Worship and the Discipline of the Sacraments was responsible for preparing the text. The Congregation is the Vatican office that the pope has charged with overseeing all matters related to the Liturgy and the sacraments. Any changes in the words of the sacramental formulas—the essential words in the celebration of each of the sacraments (either in Latin or in vernacular translations)—must be approved by the Holy Father personally. In addition, church law also gives to conferences of bishops (such as the United States Conference of Catholic Bishops) as well as individual bishops certain responsibilities with regard to the Liturgy.

What exactly is changing?

The structure of the Mass (the order of the elements, the actions of the priest celebrant, and so forth) remains unchanged in the new edition of the *Roman Missal*. However, the translation of the prayer texts will change to more closely reflect the original Latin texts. In some cases, new options for prayers may be available, and some old options may no longer be present.

Will the changes be noticeable?

In the third edition of the *Roman Missal*, almost every prayer in the Mass—those spoken by the priest and those spoken by the people—has been retranslated from the Latin to English. Some prayers now recited by memory will need to be relearned, and the familiar language of many prayers recited by the priest will change.

In preparing the new translation, the translators were asked to make the English texts conform more closely to the Latin originals and to retain traditional theological vocabulary that communicates important concepts of the faith. The language that the faithful will hear and pray is more formal and somewhat more complex than the language of ordinary conversation. It conveys rich theological concepts and retains biblical language and images.

How can I prepare for the change?

There are many ways in which you can prepare for the changes in the Mass:

✠ Make a conscious effort to participate more fully in the Mass each Sunday and holy day.
✠ Take advantage of any special catechetical sessions offered by your parish or diocese.
✠ Visit the *Roman Missal* Web site (*www.usccb.org/romanmissal*) to study the new texts and to learn more about the changes.
✠ Read the new texts of the people's parts at Mass. Begin to study them so that you will be able to pray them well when the new *Roman Missal* is implemented.
✠ Pray for a renewal of love for the Liturgy in your parish and in the Church.

What difference will these changes make in my parish?

Some of the differences will be obvious immediately. We will have to learn new musical settings for the various parts of the Mass. We will learn new words for common prayers, such as the Creed. Those of us who began saying the Mass prayers by heart long ago will need to rely on printed texts again, at least for a while. In the early months of the transition, we may find it more challenging to pray with one voice as people adjust to the new texts and gradually commit them to their hearts.

But these surface differences will give way to deeper and more significant changes. If we use the time of preparation well, we will make the changes with a deeper understanding of the Liturgy and a renewed reverence for and appreciation of the Mass. We will hear the prayers with new ears and with new hearts. Our Liturgy will be filled with new life and new spirit as we celebrate the Paschal Mystery of Christ made present for us.

Where can I turn for help in understanding these changes?

The first stop for catechesis and formation regarding these changes is your parish and diocese. All the faithful are encouraged to take advantage of parish efforts. You can attend catechetical sessions, read articles in the parish bulletin or newsletter or the diocesan newspaper, listen closely to homilies that help explain the changes, and come early to Mass to practice new musical settings for the prayers.

In addition, many dioceses, schools, universities, and retreat centers will offer programs to help people understand and appreciate the new translation. You can take advantage of these programs where possible.

The official Web site for the third edition of the *Roman Missal* is found at *www.usccb.org/romanmissal*. A variety of resources will be posted that may help you.

Catholic publishers and national organizations will publish many resources, in print and online, to help you negotiate this time of change. Check out your parish book rack or your local Catholic bookstore to see what is available.

What if I don't like the new translation?

For most people, the unfamiliar is always uncomfortable, at least at first. The more familiar the old is, the more challenging it may be to accept and embrace the new. It is completely normal to feel uncomfortable as you begin studying and reading the new texts. Taking steps to become more familiar with the texts can help a great deal. At the same time, be open to the possibility that you will find things to appreciate in the rich language of the new texts. The more you read them and study them and pray them, the more familiar and comfortable they will become and the more you will appreciate the theological depth they convey.

Taking the time to learn more about your faith, including the Mass and Scripture, can help you appreciate the new texts more fully. Using the catechetical opportunities made available by your parish and diocese can help you overcome concerns about the changes.

Finally, you can take your concerns to God in prayer. Pray for a deeper understanding of the meaning of these texts and for an open heart to grow in communion with the Church.

What can I do to make the process of change a good one for my parish?

Everyone has a role to play in preparing to use the new translations:

- ✠ Study the new texts with an open heart and an open mind so that you will be ready to use them in the Liturgy.
- ✠ Take advantage of opportunities to learn more about the new texts by attending catechetical programs and reading articles about the new texts.
- ✠ Offer to assist your pastor or parish director of religious education in preparing parish catechetical events.
- ✠ If you are a parent, teach your children the new prayers and help them to understand the changes. Encourage them to participate in the Mass fully and to learn more about their faith.
- ✠ Be very intentional about celebrating the Liturgy each Sunday and holy day. Arrive on time (or a bit early). Pray and sing with attentiveness. Stay focused on the action of the Liturgy rather than letting your mind wander. Hold the Sacrament of the Eucharist in great reverence. Finally, give thanks to God in your heart for so great a gift.

Times of change are always a challenge. But from this challenge can come a deeper appreciation of who we are as the Body of Christ, gathering to celebrate the Paschal Mystery of the Lord.

Excerpts from the English translation of the *General Instruction of the Roman Missal* ©2010, International Commission on English in the Liturgy, Inc. (ICEL). Used with permission. All rights reserved.

Scripture and the Mass

It is clear that Sacred Scripture has a revered and important place in the eucharistic Liturgy. Every Mass includes a Liturgy of the Word. The main elements of the Liturgy of the Word are biblical readings and the singing of a psalm. The Liturgy of the Word reaches its high point in the proclamation of the Gospel.

However, the use of Scripture in the Mass does not end when the Liturgy of the Word has finished. In fact, the words of Scripture flow throughout the prayers of the Mass. One of the goals of the new translation of the *Missal* was to make clearer the links between the prayers of the Mass and the text of Scripture. Some of the most noticeable changes reflect the words of the Bible more clearly. Let's take a look at some of these changes.

A BIBLICAL GREETING

At several points in the Mass, the priest or deacon and the people engage in the following dialogue:

> Priest or Deacon: The Lord be with you.
> All: And with your spirit. (*The Order of Mass*, 2)

The first words come from a greeting of Boaz, the great-grandfather of King David: "Boaz . . . said to the harvesters, 'The Lord be with you!' and they replied, 'The Lord bless you!'" (Ru 2:4). The people's response reflects the language of St. Paul. In Galatians, he says, "The grace of our Lord Jesus Christ be with your spirit, brothers. Amen" (Gal 6:18); the Second Letter to Timothy closes with a similar wish: "The Lord be with your spirit" (2 Tm 4:22). The Letter to the Philippians ends with "The grace of the Lord Jesus Christ be with your spirit" (Phil 4:23).

The new language, though a bit unfamiliar to our ears, more directly reflects the biblical understanding that, through Baptism, the Spirit of God dwells in us and unites us as one Body in Christ.

WELCOMING THE LORD

Immediately before coming forward to receive the Lord in Holy Communion, we welcome the Lord:

> Lord, I am not worthy
> that you should enter under my roof,
> but only say the word
> and my soul shall be healed. (*The Order of Mass*, 132)

This prayer quotes the words of the centurion who asked Jesus to cure his servant. He would not presume to ask Jesus to come to his home. He trusted in the authority of Jesus' healing word, saying: "Lord, I am not worthy to have you enter under my roof; only say the word and my servant will be healed" (Mt 8:8; see Lk 7:6-7). This new phrasing reminds us that, in receiving Holy Communion, we are to emulate the centurion's humility and faith.

FOR THE MANY

One of the most notable changes will come in the words that the priest speaks in consecrating the wine as the Blood of Christ:

> Take this, all of you, and drink from it:
> for this is the chalice of my Blood,
> the Blood of the new and eternal covenant,
> which will be poured out for you and for many
> for the forgiveness of sins. (*The Order of Mass*, 90)

The newly translated text more closely reflects the scriptural accounts of the Last Supper: "Then he took a cup, gave thanks, and gave it to them, saying, 'Drink from it, all of you, for this is my blood of the covenant, which will be shed on behalf of many for the forgiveness of sins'" (Mt 26:27-28). Much attention has focused on a single change in this text: from "for all" to "for many." This change is unique to the English language. Other languages, including Spanish, French, and German, have already been using language that more closely reflects Jesus' words at the Last Supper.

This new text does not mean that God's love is limited or that only some may be saved. Rather, it reflects the fact that human beings may choose to accept the grace of salvation and live their lives in the light of this grace.

DEEPER UNDERSTANDING

If we recognize the biblical references that underlie the liturgical texts, we will have a fuller understanding of their meaning. For example, Eucharistic Prayer I includes the following passage:

> Be pleased to look upon these offerings
> with a serene and kindly countenance,
> and to accept them,
> as you were pleased to accept
> the gifts of your servant Abel the just,
> the sacrifice of Abraham, our father in faith,
> and the offering of your high priest Melchizedek,
> a holy sacrifice, a spotless victim. (*The Order of Mass*, 93)

If we do not know who Abel (Gn 4:4) and Melchizedek (Gn 14:18-20) are and if we do not understand the importance of Abraham's sacrifice (Gn 15:7-21; 22:1-14), we will not fully appreciate the concept of sacrifice and how our celebration of the eucharistic sacrifice ties us to our ancestors in the faith, from the very beginning.

THE WORD OF GOD IN SCRIPTURE AND THE EUCHARIST

Translating the liturgical texts with a close eye to their correspondence with the texts of Scripture can help us to develop a greater appreciation of the close links between the prayers of the Mass and Sacred Scripture. These close links can help draw us more deeply into the theological meaning of the texts.

For example, before the Communion Rite, the priest breaks the Host and shows it to the people, saying:

> Behold the Lamb of God,
>   behold him who takes away the sins of the world.
> Blessed are those called to the supper of the Lamb.
> (*The Order of Mass*, 132)

The first part of this prayer echoes the words of John the Baptist, heralding the coming of the Christ: "The next day he [John] saw Jesus coming toward him and said, 'Behold, the Lamb of God, who takes away the sin of the world'" (Jn 1:29). In the same way, we who are united in the Body of Christ in the Sacrament of Baptism and strengthened in the Eucharist are called to point others to Jesus through our words and actions.

The second part of this prayer reflects the words of the Book of Revelation: "Then the angel said to me, 'Write this: Blessed are those who have been called to the wedding feast of the Lamb'" (Rev 19:9). In this prayer, we are not rejoicing that we may receive the Eucharist. Instead, we rejoice for those who have been found worthy to share in the heavenly Liturgy, the supper of the Lamb, and we pray that one day, we may join them in the everlasting life of the Kingdom of God.

CONCLUSION

By delving more deeply into the scriptural background of the Mass, we come to know more closely Jesus, the Word of God made flesh, whose Paschal Mystery we celebrate.

REFERENCE

Excerpts from the English translation of the *Roman Missal* ©2010, International Commission on English in the Liturgy, Inc. (ICEL). All rights reserved.

Scripture texts used in this work are taken from the *New American Bible*, copyright © 1991, 1986, and 1970 by the Confraternity of Christian Doctrine, Washington, DC 20017 and are used by permission of the copyright owner. All rights reserved.

APPENDIX E

OTHER RESOURCES FROM THE USCCB

Book of Readings on the Eucharist

Pastoral Liturgy Series 3

Formally proclaimed and actively fulfilled, the Eucharist is the source and summit of Christian life. The reflections in the *Book of Readings on the Eucharist* address the relationship between the Eucharist and various dimensions of Catholic practice, life, and belief. The essays are designed to promote a deeper appreciation and love for the Eucharist in the hearts, minds, and souls of everyone from cradle Catholics to neophytes. Each chapter includes reflection or discussion questions that can be used in various settings, such as personal prayer or mystagogy.
No. 5-706, 114 pp.

Compendium on the Eucharist

A collection of important sources including doctrinal selections from key documents, liturgical text, and prayers. The appendices include an excerpt from the *Imitation of Christ* and the *Code of Canon Law* from the Latin and Eastern Churches.
No. 7-114, coming soon

The Eucharist

Spiritual Thoughts Series

As we remember Christ's sacrifice for us, the Holy Father discusses the Sacrament of the Eucharist and how it unites us with the living God and allows us to freely give of ourselves to others. The Eucharist is an exchange between God and humanity that brings us closer to him and reminds us of the purpose for our lives. The heart of the Church and the heart of the life of every Christian is essentially eucharistic in that it carries Christ within.
No. 7-084, 112 pp.

Following Christ

Spiritual Thoughts Series

What is our responsibility as followers of Christ? How do we show the love that God so completely shows us? Find inspiration for daily Christian living as you read *Following Christ*. In excerpts from his writings, speeches, and homilies, Pope Benedict XVI discusses how to develop a relationship with Christ and become more effective disciples.
No. 7-056, 132 pp.

The Priesthood

Spiritual Thoughts Series

Pope Benedict XVI discusses the mission and purpose of the priesthood. The Holy Father states that the essence of the priesthood is consecration, sacrifice, and the giving over of one's self to God. Intimacy with God, in relationship and dialogue, empowers the central task of the priest: to bring God to men and women and to remind them of the ultimate purpose of their lives.

No. 7-086, 83 pp.

Essential Guide to Saints and Seasons

This small book provides an introduction to liturgical time including Sunday, the liturgical seasons, and the feasts of the Lord and of the saints that we celebrate through the year.

No. 7-124, coming soon

The Church's Common Treasure

Roman Missal, Third Edition

Articles that address the following questions have been developed by the USCCB and can be found on the *Roman Missal* Web site: *www.usccb.org/romanmissal.*

⊞ Why are we going to have changes in the *Roman Missal*? How often does the *Roman Missal* change? Why is it changing now? Why are we using words that seem obsolete?

⊞ What are the key changes in the responses of the congregation? Why are they being made? How will parishioners know what to say?

⊞ Who are the new saints in the *Roman Missal*? Why were they added? Can priests add others when they want to?

⊞ The *Roman Missal* seems to go from an informal speech rhythm to a formal pattern of speech. Is this intentional? Why?

⊞ There is a saying that "every translator is a traitor." What are the challenges that translators meet? How has this affected the liturgical translations?

⊞ Will the changes affect other church ministers, e.g., lectors, extraordinary ministers of Holy Communion, and musicians? Will these changes affect church music?

⊞ Why is the Mass so important to Catholicism? How does it differ from other church services? Why are there so many mentions of "we" rather than "I" in the Mass? Why do changes in the Mass touch people so deeply?

⊞ What can Catholics do to improve appreciation of the Mass? What is the relationship between the Mass and my daily life?

⊞ The priest offering Mass faces the most challenges in implementing these changes. What does he need to do to get ready for the *Roman Missal*?

⊞ Why are there different Eucharistic Prayers?

⊞ What is the *Roman Missal*? Why should I care about it?

No. 7-158, coming soon

APPENDIX F

RESOURCES FROM OTHER CATHOLIC PUBLISHERS AND NATIONAL ORGANIZATIONS

Catholic Book Publishing

Roman Missal (Large size, leather edition, with tabs and ribbon markers)

Roman Missal (Large size, cloth edition, with tabs and ribbon markers)

Roman Missal (Small size, cloth edition, with tabs and ribbon markers)

These resources may be ordered from Catholic Book Publishing online at *www.catholicbookpublishing.com*; by phone at 877-CATBOOK (228-2665) (toll-free only in the continental United States; outside the continental United States, please call 973-890-2400); by fax at 800-890-1844 (toll-free only in continental United States; outside the continental United States, please fax to 973-890-2410); or by mail at 77 West End Road, Totowa, NJ 07512. Only Visa and MasterCard accepted.

Federation of Diocesan Liturgical Commissions

With One Voice: Translation and Implementation of the Third Edition of the Roman Missal
Includes essays on liturgical leadership and change; the implementation of the *Roman Missal, Third Edition*; liturgical participation; and ritual texts. Authors include Bishop Gerald Kicanas; Rev. John J. M. Foster; Rev. Mark Francis, CSV; and Rev. Paul Turner.

Bulletin Inserts

Why a New Translation?
Question-and-answer format for parish distribution. Includes accompanying background about translation issues for parish leadership.

Liturgical Participation of God's People
The implementation of the *Roman Missal* is a time to re-explore the basic principles of liturgical participation.

Where Do Liturgical Books Come From?

The missal that is used for Mass: where does it come from? Provides a brief description of the process by which the *Roman Missal* in English comes into existence.

Ritual Dialogues of the Mass

The celebration of Mass is structured by a number of short dialogues between the presiding priest and the liturgical congregation. What are these about?

Joining Together in Prayer

Provides mystagogical reflections on the *Gloria*, Creed, *Sanctus* (Holy, Holy), Memorial Acclamation, Our Father, and *Agnus Dei* (Lamb of God).

Other Types of Resources

The Mystery of Faith: A Study of the Structural Elements of the Order of the Mass

This book provides a detailed, step-by-step guide to all the various parts of the Mass and how they fit together.

Packaged or Boxed Workshops

These include leader's notes, PowerPoint presentations, discussion outlines, and Q&As. One set is for clergy; another is for parish ministers or liturgical ministers. Both are preceded by a video presentation by Bishop Arthur J. Serratelli introducing the *Roman Missal* and its translation.

Audio CDs Presenting the New Translations

This oral presentation of the newly translated prayers from the *Roman Missal* will help celebrants to work on the sentence structure and cadence of the translation.

Parish Catechesis in a Box

This boxed plan is designed to be used with parish assemblies. It consists of bulletin inserts, homily hints, brief announcements before the Liturgy, and material for parish Web sites.

To order, contact Federation of Diocesan Liturgical Commissions, 415 Michigan Avenue NE, Suite 70, Washington, DC 20017; *www.fdlc.org*; e-mail: *publications@fdlc.org*; phone: 202-635-6990; fax: 202-529-2452.

Liturgy Training Publications

Guide to the Revised Order of Mass by Paul Turner

Introducing the Revised Roman Missal by Rev. Robert L. Tuzik, PhD

Revised Roman Missal: Understanding the Revised Mass Texts by Paul Turner

- ⌘ Why and How Are the Revised Mass Texts Being Revised?
- ⌘ The Introductory Rites
- ⌘ The Gloria and the Liturgy of the Word
- ⌘ The Profession of Faith
- ⌘ The Liturgy of the Eucharist
- ⌘ The Eucharistic Prayer
- ⌘ The Mystery of Faith
- ⌘ The Communion and Concluding Rites

Revised Roman Missal: Understanding the Revised Mass Texts Series Pack by Paul Turner

To order, customers can call toll-free 800-933-1800 or visit us at *www.LTP.org*.

Magnificat

The MAGNIFICAT New Missal Companion

A companion to help people understand what the new translation of the Missal is all about and what it means for them. As low as $0.99 per copy (generous discount for bulk orders). Available May 2011. To order and for more info: *www.magnificat.com* or call 970-416-6670.